School Rumble

Jin Kobayashi

TRANSLATED AND ADAPTED BY
William Flanagan

LETTERED BY
Michaelis/Carpelis Design

LONDON

Published in the United Kingdom by Tanoshimi in 2008

1 3 5 7 9 10 8 6 4 2

School Rumble, Volume 8 is a work of fiction. Names, characters, places and incidents are the products of the author's imagination or are used fictitiously. Any resemblance to actual events, locales, or persons, living or dead, is entirely coincidental.

First published in Japan by Kodansha Ltd., Tokyo in 2004

Published by arrangement with Kodansha Ltd., Tokyo and with Del Rey, an imprint of Random House Inc., New York

Tanoshimi
The Random House Group Limited
20 Vauxhall Bridge Road, London, SW1V 2SA

www.tanoshimi.tv
www.rbooks.co.uk

Addresses for companies within The Random House Group Limited can be found at:
www.randomhouse.co.uk

Random House Group Limited Reg. No. 954009

A CIP catalogue record for this book is available from the British Library

ISBN 9780099506447

The Random House Group Limited makes every effort to ensure that the papers used in its books are made from trees that have been legally sourced from well-managed and credibly certified forests. Our paper procurement policy can be found at: www.randomhouse.co.uk/paper.htm

Printed and bound in Germany by GGP Media GmbH, Pößneck

Translator and adaptor – William Flanagan
Lettering – Michaelis/Carpelis Design

Honorifics Explained

Throughout the Tanoshimi Manga books, you will find Japanese honorifics left intact in the translations. For those not familiar with how the Japanese use honorifics and, more important, how they differ from English honorifics, we present this brief overview.

Politeness has always been a critical facet of Japanese culture. Ever since the feudal era, when Japan was a highly stratified society, use of honorifics—which can be defined as polite speech that indicates relationship or status—has played an essential role in the Japanese language. When addressing someone in Japanese, an honorific usually takes the form of a suffix attached to one's name (example: "Asuna-san"), is used as a title at the end of one's name, or appears in place of the name itself (example: "Negi-sensei," or simply "Sensei!").

Honorifics can be expressions of respect or endearment. In the context of manga and anime, honorifics give insight into the nature of the relationship between characters. Many English translations leave out these important honorifics and therefore distort the feel of the original Japanese. Because Japanese honorifics contain nuances that English honorifics lack, it is our policy at Tanoshimi not to translate them. Here, instead, is a guide to some of the honorifics you may encounter in Tanoshimi Manga.

-san: This is the most common honorific and is equivalent to Mr., Miss, Ms., or Mrs. It is the all-purpose honorific and can be used in any situation where politeness is required.

-sama: This is one level higher than "-san" and is used to confer great respect.

-dono: This comes from the word "tono" which means "lord." It is an even higher level than "-sama" and confers utmost respect.

-kun: This suffix is used at the end of boys' names to express familiarity or endearment. It is also sometimes used by men among friends, or when addressing someone younger or of a lower station.

-chan: This is used to express endearment, mostly toward girls. It is also used for little boys, pets, and even among lovers. It gives a sense of childish cuteness.

Bozu: This is an informal way to refer to a boy, similar to the English terms "kid".

Sempai/Senpai: This title suggests that the addressee is one's senior in a group or organization. It is most often used in a school setting, where underclassmen refer to their upperclassmen as "sempai." It can also be used in the workplace, such as when a newer employee addresses an employee who has seniority in the company.

Kohai: This is the opposite of "sempai" and is used toward underclassmen in school or newcomers in the workplace. It connotes that the addressee is of a lower station.

Sensei: Literally meaning "one who has come before," this title is used for teachers, doctors, or masters of any profession or art.

Onee-san/Onii-san: Normally older siblings are not called by name but rather by the title of older sister (Onee-san) or older brother (Onii-san). Depending on the relationship, "-chan" or "-sama" can also be used instead of "-san." However, this honorific can also be used with someone unrelated when the relationship resembles that of siblings.

-[blank]: This is usually forgotten in these lists, but it is perhaps the most significant difference between Japanese and English. The lack of honorific means that the speaker has permission to address the person in a very intimate way. Usually, only family, spouses, or very close friends have this kind of permission. Known as *yobisute*, it can be gratifying when someone who has earned the intimacy starts to call one by one's name without an honorific. But when that intimacy hasn't been earned, it can be very insulting.

Cultural Note

To preserve some of the humor found in *School Rumble*, we have elected to keep Japanese names in their original Japanese order—that is to say, with the family name first, followed by the personal name. So when you hear the name Tsukamoto Tenma, Tenma is just one member of the Tsukamoto family.

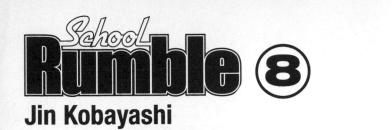

School Rumble 8

Jin Kobayashi

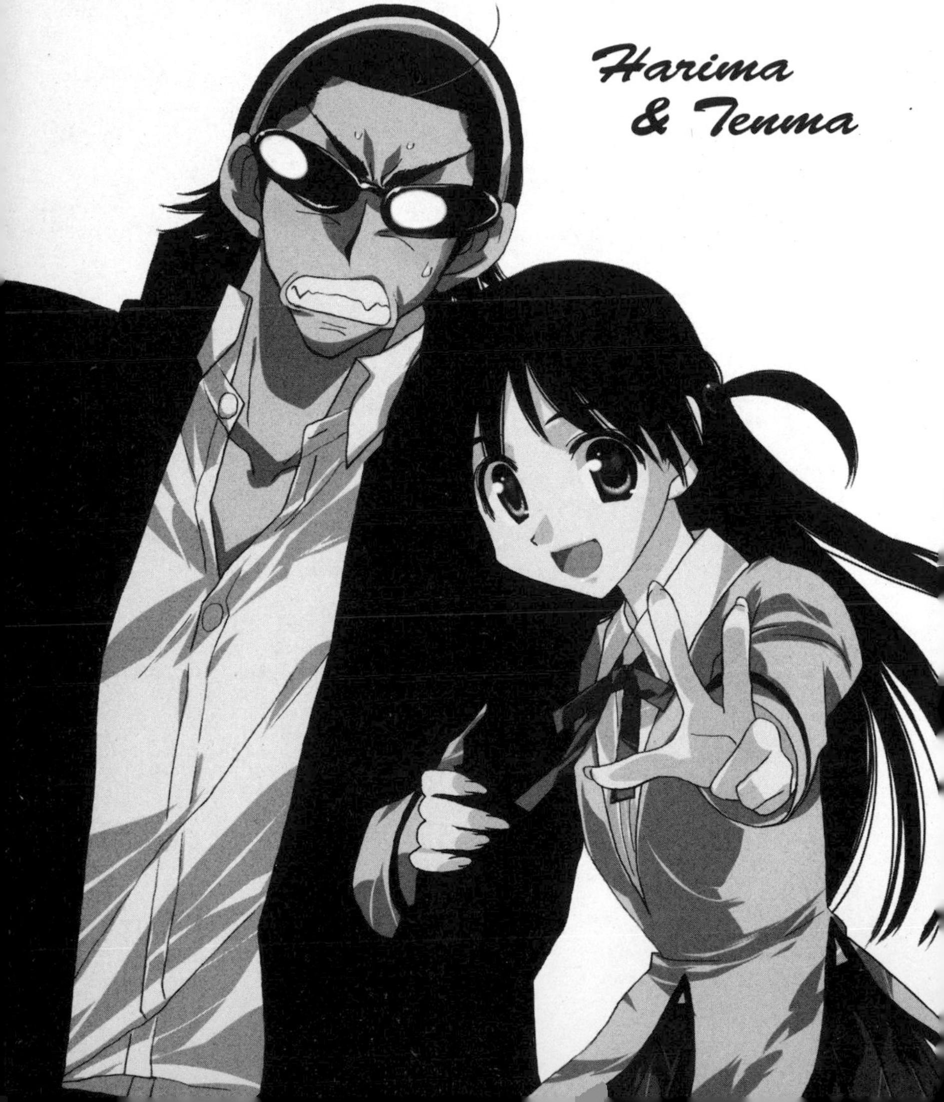
Harima
& Tenma

Contents

#97 TWO FOR THE ROAD 003

#98 THE BIRTHDAY PARTY 013

#99 THE TRUE-HEARTED 023

#100 GELOSIA 030

#101 TOO HOT TO HANDLE 038

#102 JOHNNY GOT HIS GUN 049

#103 THE DOGS OF WAR 059

#104 THE ULTIMATE THRILL 073

#105 QUICK 085

#106 LA TRAVESTIE 096

#107 WHISPERS IN THE DARK 106

#108 TRULY, MADLY, DEEPLY 117

♭21 NUIT DOCILE 129

♭22 THE SECRET GARDEN 137

♭23 CALIFORNIA MAN 145

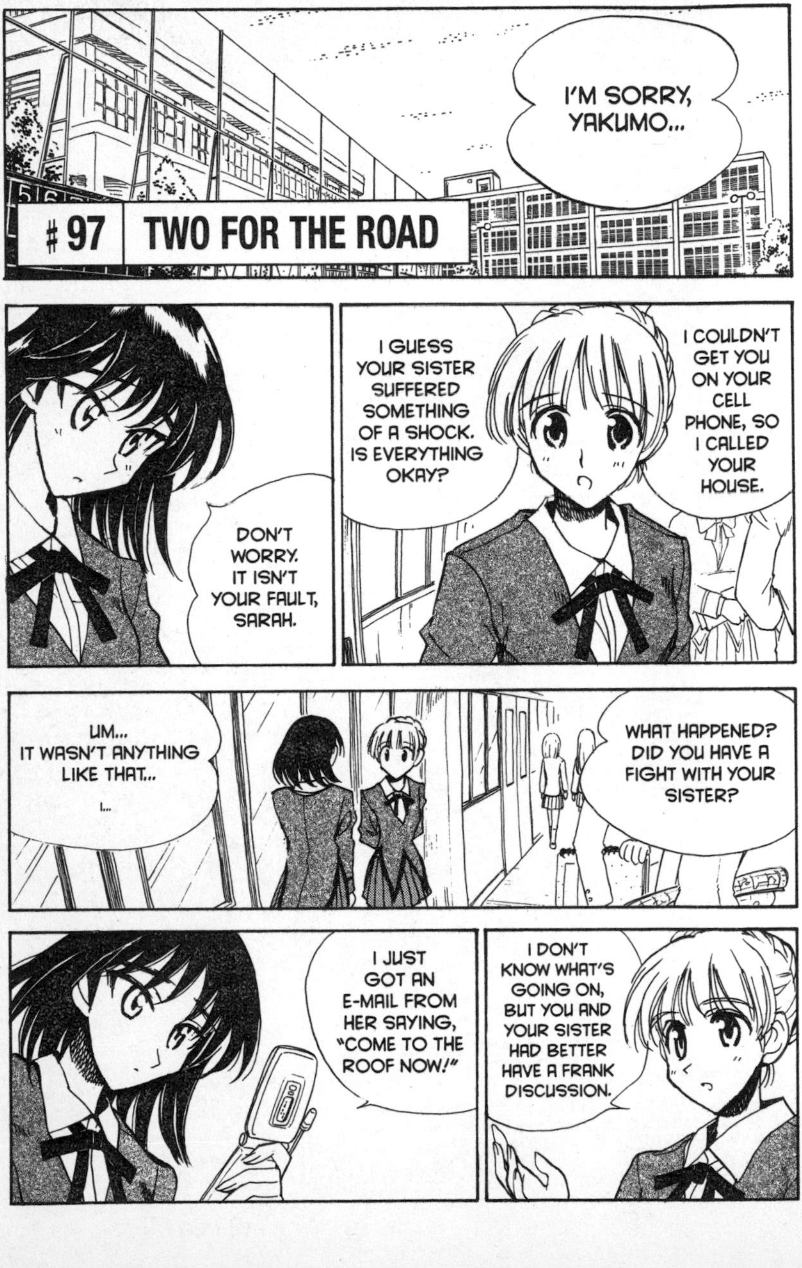

97 TWO FOR THE ROAD
I'M SORRY, YAKUMO...
I COULDN'T GET YOU ON YOUR CELL PHONE, SO I CALLED YOUR HOUSE.
I GUESS YOUR SISTER SUFFERED SOMETHING OF A SHOCK. IS EVERYTHING OKAY?
DON'T WORRY. IT ISN'T YOUR FAULT, SARAH.
WHAT HAPPENED? DID YOU HAVE A FIGHT WITH YOUR SISTER?
UM... IT WASN'T ANYTHING LIKE THAT... I...
I DON'T KNOW WHAT'S GOING ON, BUT YOU AND YOUR SISTER HAD BETTER HAVE A FRANK DISCUSSION.
I JUST GOT AN E-MAIL FROM HER SAYING, "COME TO THE ROOF NOW!"

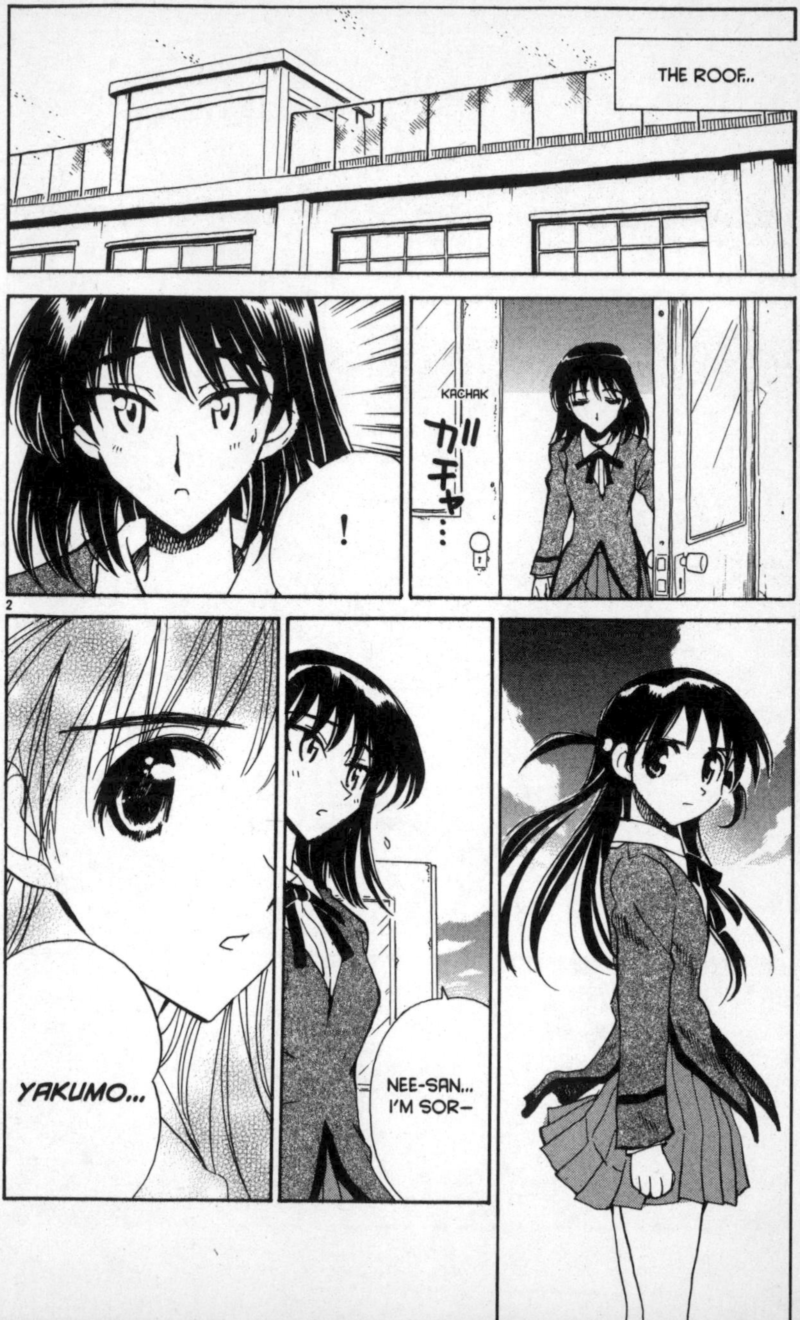
THE ROOF...
KACHAK
ガチャ...
!
NEE-SAN...
I'M SOR–
YAKUMO...

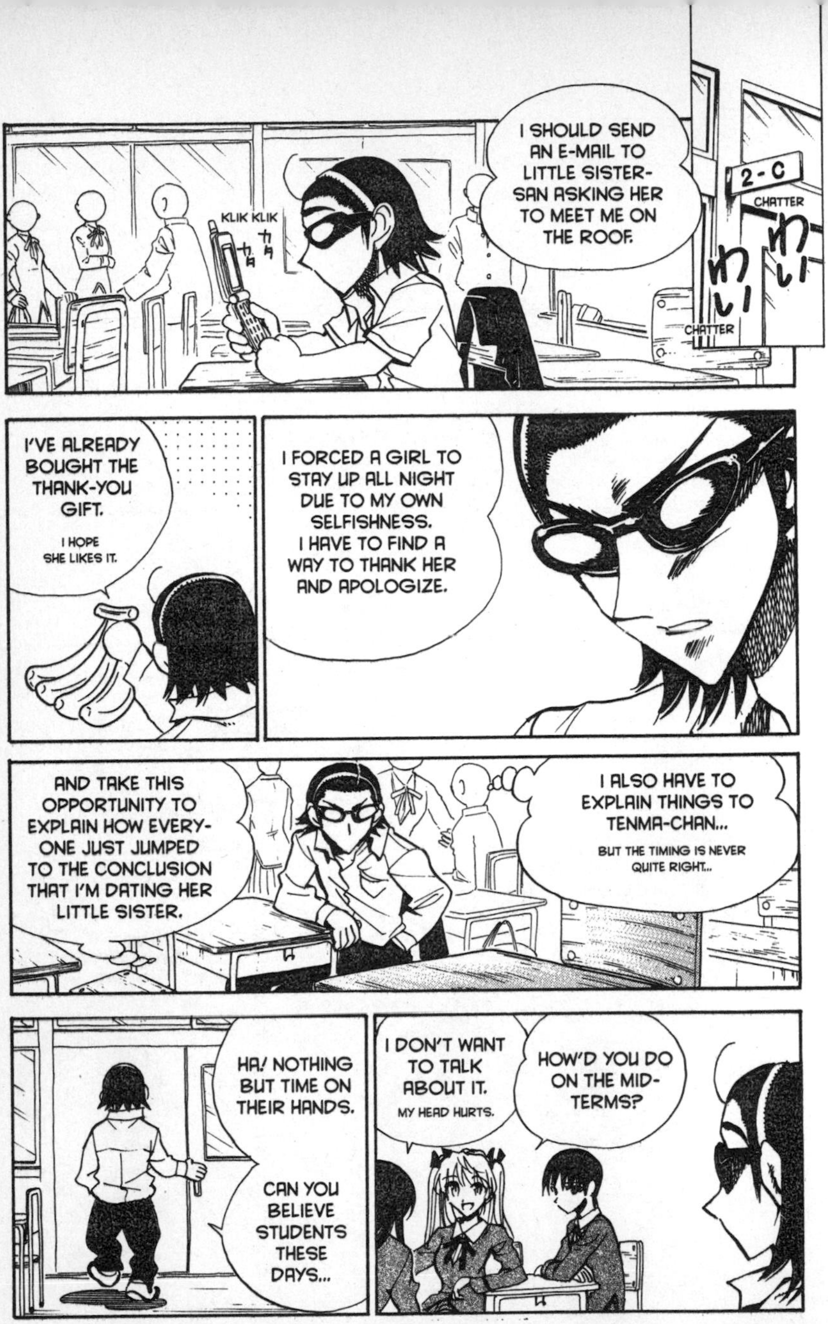
2-C
CHATTER
わい
わい
CHATTER
I SHOULD SEND AN E-MAIL TO LITTLE SISTER-SAN ASKING HER TO MEET ME ON THE ROOF.
KLIK KLIK
カタ
カタ
I FORCED A GIRL TO STAY UP ALL NIGHT DUE TO MY OWN SELFISHNESS. I HAVE TO FIND A WAY TO THANK HER AND APOLOGIZE.
I'VE ALREADY BOUGHT THE THANK-YOU GIFT.
I HOPE SHE LIKES IT.
I ALSO HAVE TO EXPLAIN THINGS TO TENMA-CHAN...
BUT THE TIMING IS NEVER QUITE RIGHT...
AND TAKE THIS OPPORTUNITY TO EXPLAIN HOW EVERY-ONE JUST JUMPED TO THE CONCLUSION THAT I'M DATING HER LITTLE SISTER.
HOW'D YOU DO ON THE MID-TERMS?
I DON'T WANT TO TALK ABOUT IT.
MY HEAD HURTS.
HA! NOTHING BUT TIME ON THEIR HANDS.
CAN YOU BELIEVE STUDENTS THESE DAYS...

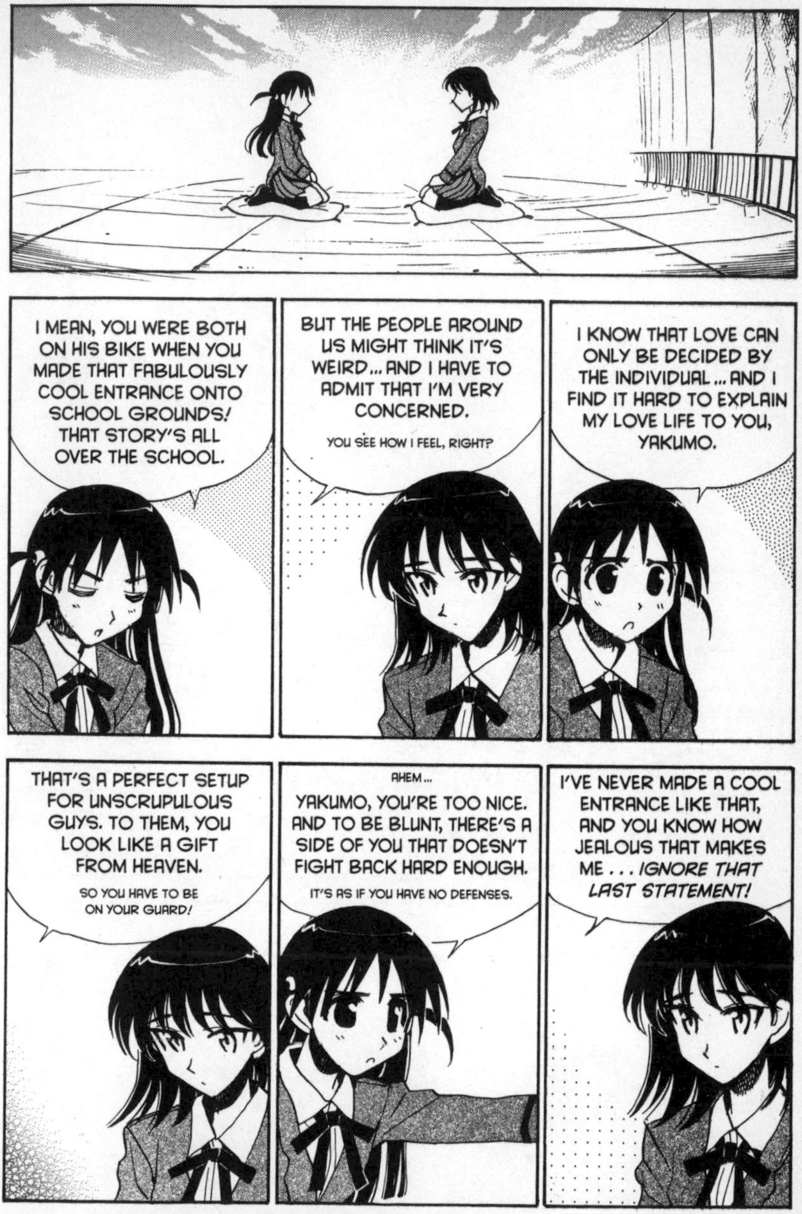
I KNOW THAT LOVE CAN ONLY BE DECIDED BY THE INDIVIDUAL ... AND I FIND IT HARD TO EXPLAIN MY LOVE LIFE TO YOU, YAKUMO.
BUT THE PEOPLE AROUND US MIGHT THINK IT'S WEIRD... AND I HAVE TO ADMIT THAT I'M VERY CONCERNED.
YOU SEE HOW I FEEL, RIGHT?
I MEAN, YOU WERE BOTH ON HIS BIKE WHEN YOU MADE THAT FABULOUSLY COOL ENTRANCE ONTO SCHOOL GROUNDS! THAT STORY'S ALL OVER THE SCHOOL.
I'VE NEVER MADE A COOL ENTRANCE LIKE THAT, AND YOU KNOW HOW JEALOUS THAT MAKES ME . . . *IGNORE THAT LAST STATEMENT!*
AHEM...
YAKUMO, YOU'RE TOO NICE. AND TO BE BLUNT, THERE'S A SIDE OF YOU THAT DOESN'T FIGHT BACK HARD ENOUGH.
IT'S AS IF YOU HAVE NO DEFENSES.
THAT'S A PERFECT SETUP FOR UNSCRUPULOUS GUYS. TO THEM, YOU LOOK LIKE A GIFT FROM HEAVEN.
SO YOU HAVE TO BE ON YOUR GUARD!

Zabuton Cushions Supplied by the Tea Club.

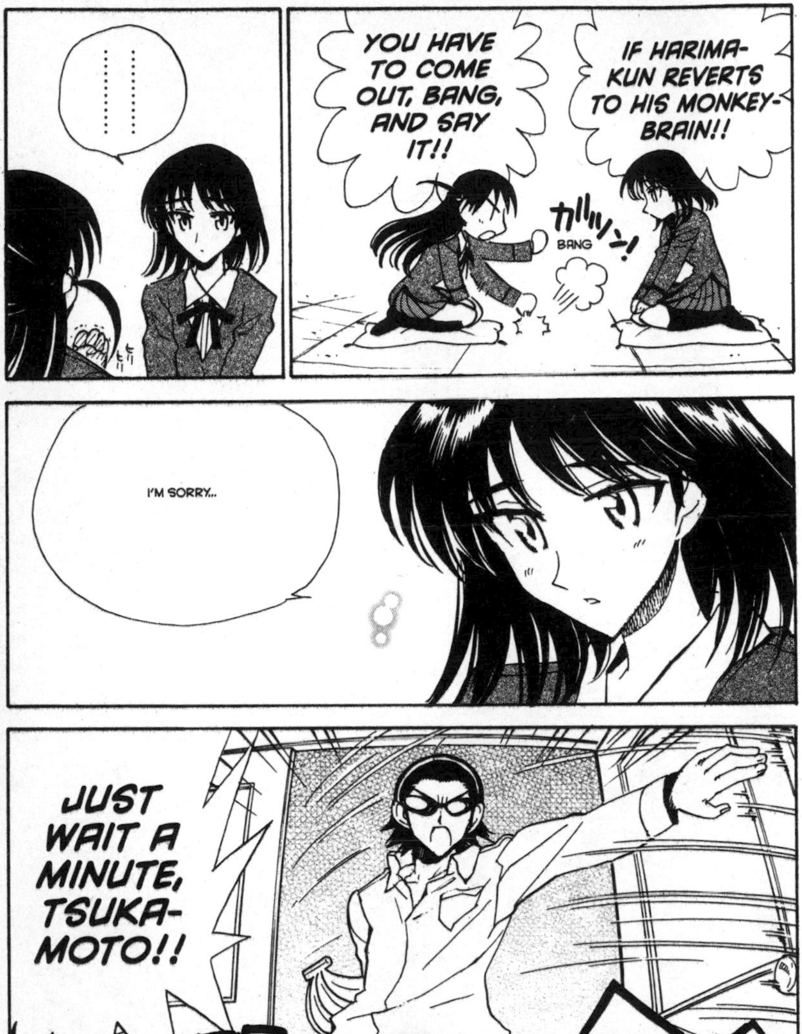
IF HARIMA-KUN REVERTS TO HIS MONKEY-BRAIN!!
YOU HAVE TO COME OUT, BANG, AND SAY IT!!
BANG
......
I'M SORRY...
JUST WAIT A MINUTE, TSUKAMOTO!!
BAMM

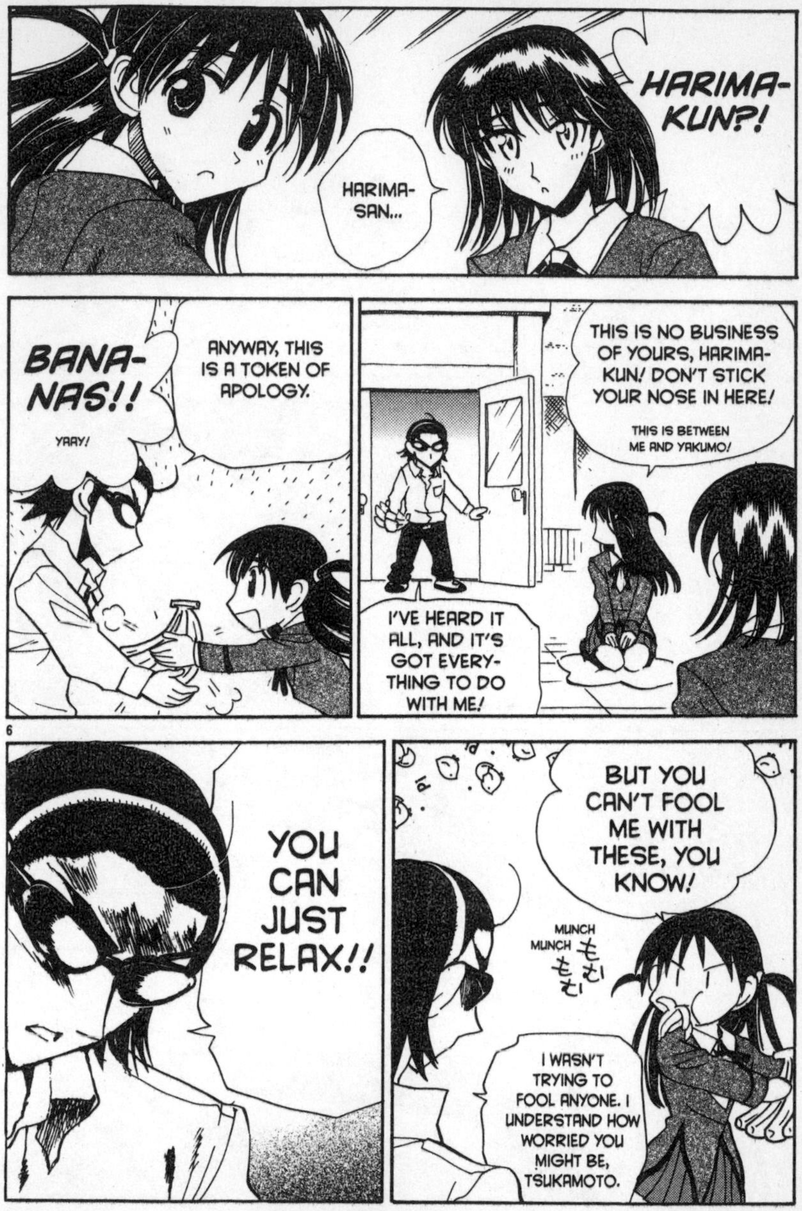
HARIMA-KUN?!
HARIMA-SAN...
THIS IS NO BUSINESS OF YOURS, HARIMA-KUN! DON'T STICK YOUR NOSE IN HERE!
THIS IS BETWEEN ME AND YAKUMO!
I'VE HEARD IT ALL, AND IT'S GOT EVERYTHING TO DO WITH ME!
ANYWAY, THIS IS A TOKEN OF APOLOGY.
BANANAS!!
YAAY!
6
BUT YOU CAN'T FOOL ME WITH THESE, YOU KNOW!
MUNCH MUNCH もむもむ
I WASN'T TRYING TO FOOL ANYONE. I UNDERSTAND HOW WORRIED YOU MIGHT BE, TSUKAMOTO.
YOU CAN JUST RELAX!!

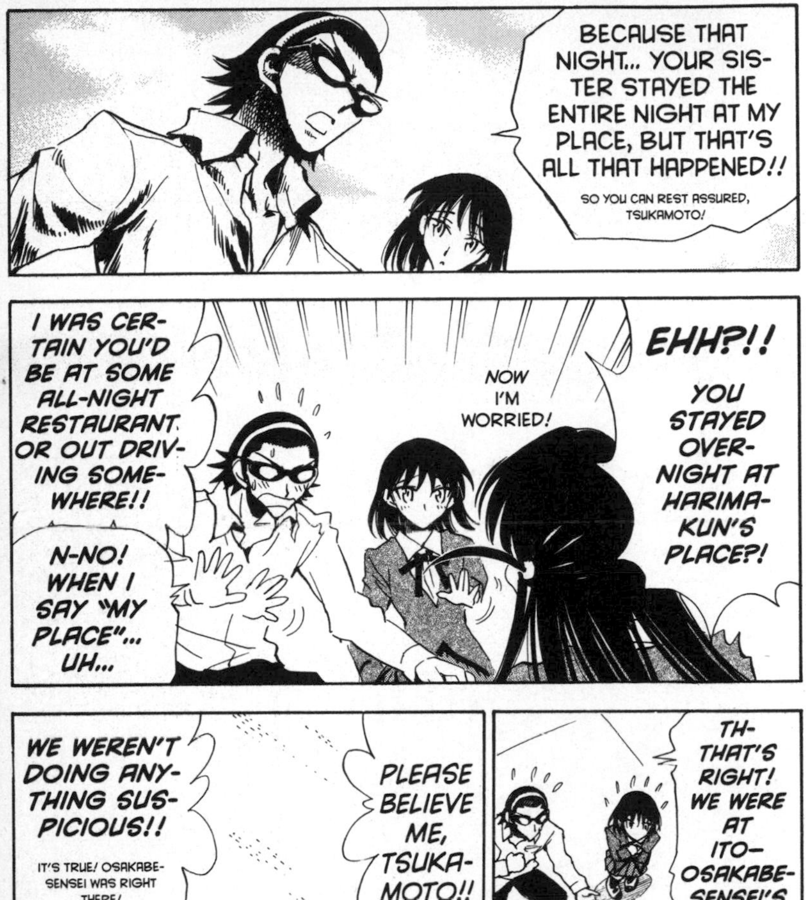
BECAUSE THAT NIGHT... YOUR SISTER STAYED THE ENTIRE NIGHT AT MY PLACE, BUT THAT'S ALL THAT HAPPENED!!
SO YOU CAN REST ASSURED, TSUKAMOTO!
EHH?!!
YOU STAYED OVERNIGHT AT HARIMA-KUN'S PLACE?!
NOW I'M WORRIED!
I WAS CERTAIN YOU'D BE AT SOME ALL-NIGHT RESTAURANT OR OUT DRIVING SOMEWHERE!!
N-NO! WHEN I SAY "MY PLACE"... UH...
TH-THAT'S RIGHT! WE WERE AT ITO-OSAKABE-SENSEI'S PLACE!
ITOKO-SENSEI'S PLACE?!
THAT SOUNDS LIKE A LIE!
PLEASE BELIEVE ME, TSUKAMOTO!!
WE WEREN'T DOING ANYTHING SUSPICIOUS!!
IT'S TRUE! OSAKABE-SENSEI WAS RIGHT THERE!
WE NEVER ONCE LEFT THE DESK!
YEAH, NEVER LEFT THE DESK!!

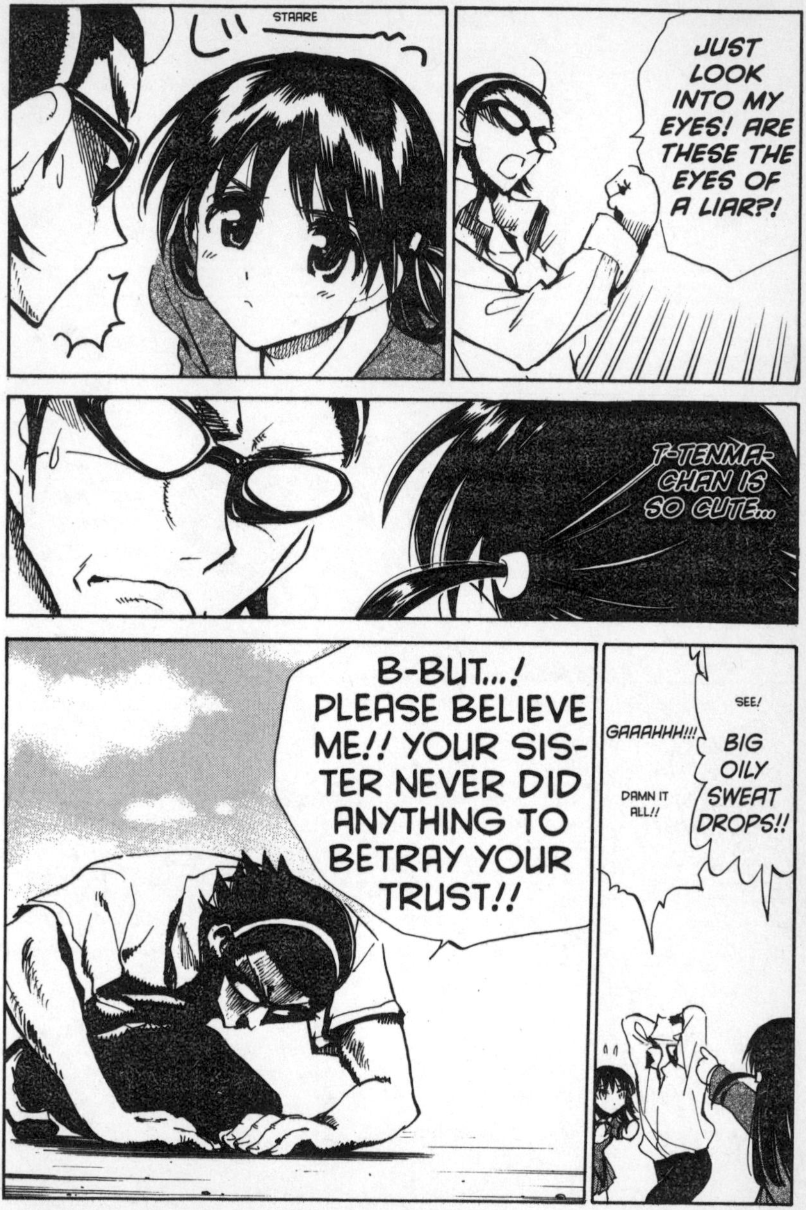
JUST LOOK INTO MY EYES! ARE THESE THE EYES OF A LIAR?!
STAARE
T-TENMA-CHAN IS SO CUTE...
SEE!
BIG OILY SWEAT DROPS!!
GAAAHHH!!!
DAMN IT ALL!!
B-BUT...! PLEASE BELIEVE ME!! YOUR SIS-TER NEVER DID ANYTHING TO BETRAY YOUR TRUST!!

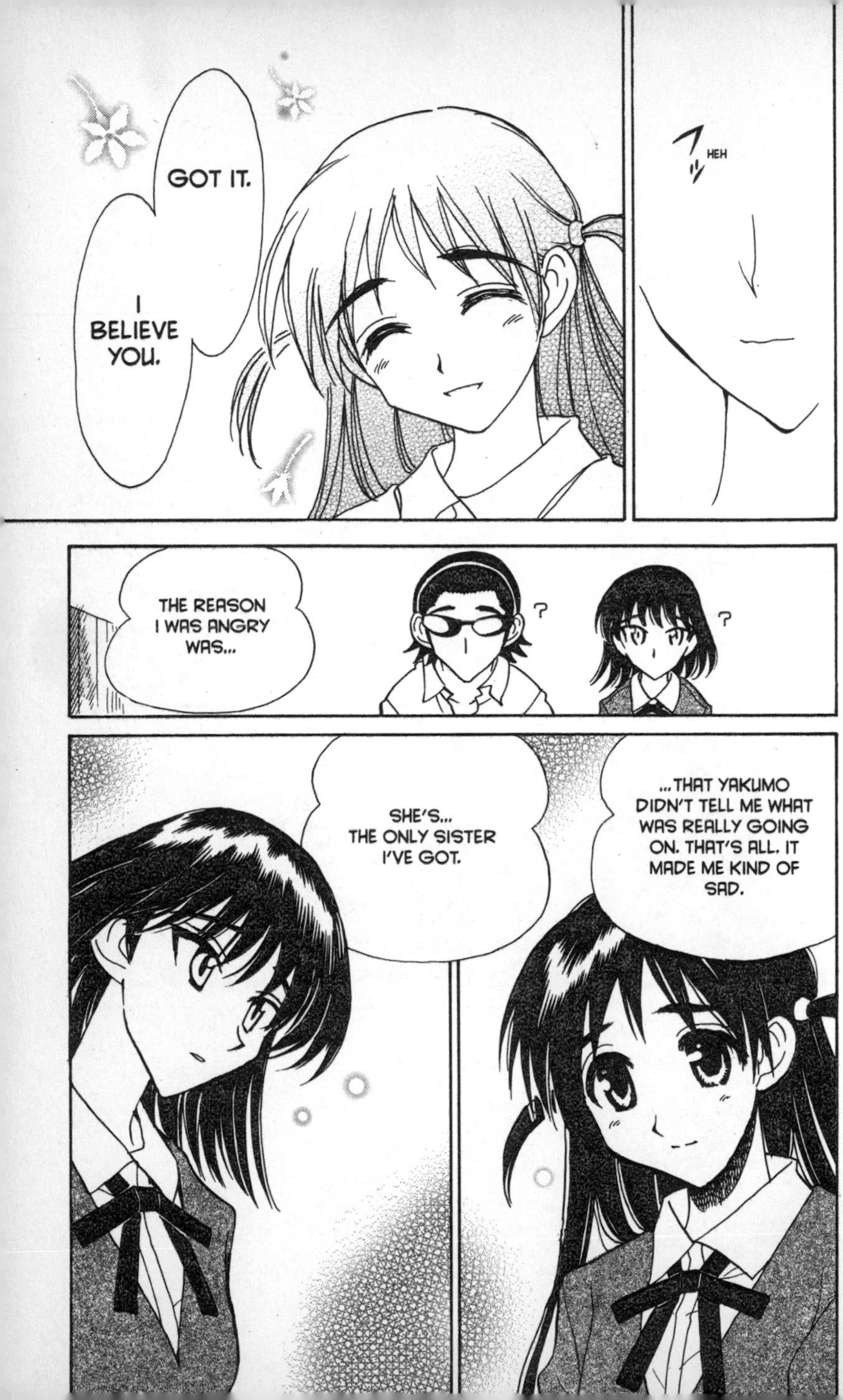
HEH
GOT IT.
I BELIEVE YOU.
THE REASON I WAS ANGRY WAS...
...THAT YAKUMO DIDN'T TELL ME WHAT WAS REALLY GOING ON. THAT'S ALL. IT MADE ME KIND OF SAD.
SHE'S... THE ONLY SISTER I'VE GOT.

And the Misconception Triangle Is Complete.

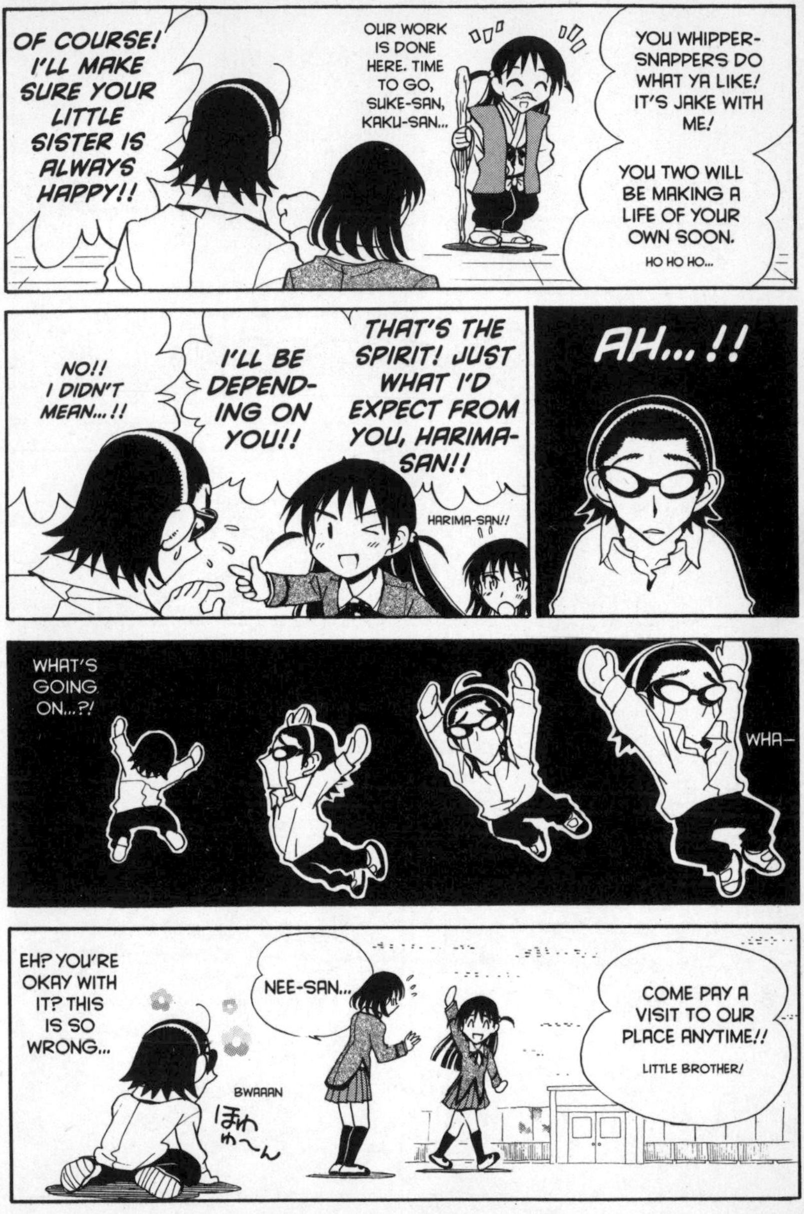
YOU WHIPPER-SNAPPERS DO WHAT YA LIKE! IT'S JAKE WITH ME!
YOU TWO WILL BE MAKING A LIFE OF YOUR OWN SOON.
HO HO HO...
OUR WORK IS DONE HERE. TIME TO GO, SUKE-SAN, KAKU-SAN...
OF COURSE! I'LL MAKE SURE YOUR LITTLE SISTER IS ALWAYS HAPPY!!
AH...!!
THAT'S THE SPIRIT! JUST WHAT I'D EXPECT FROM YOU, HARIMA-SAN!!
I'LL BE DEPENDING ON YOU!!
NO!! I DIDN'T MEAN...!!
HARIMA-SAN!!
WHA-
WHAT'S GOING ON...?!
COME PAY A VISIT TO OUR PLACE ANYTIME!!
LITTLE BROTHER!
NEE-SAN...
EH? YOU'RE OKAY WITH IT? THIS IS SO WRONG...
BWAAAN
ほわゎ〜ん

97 ....Fin

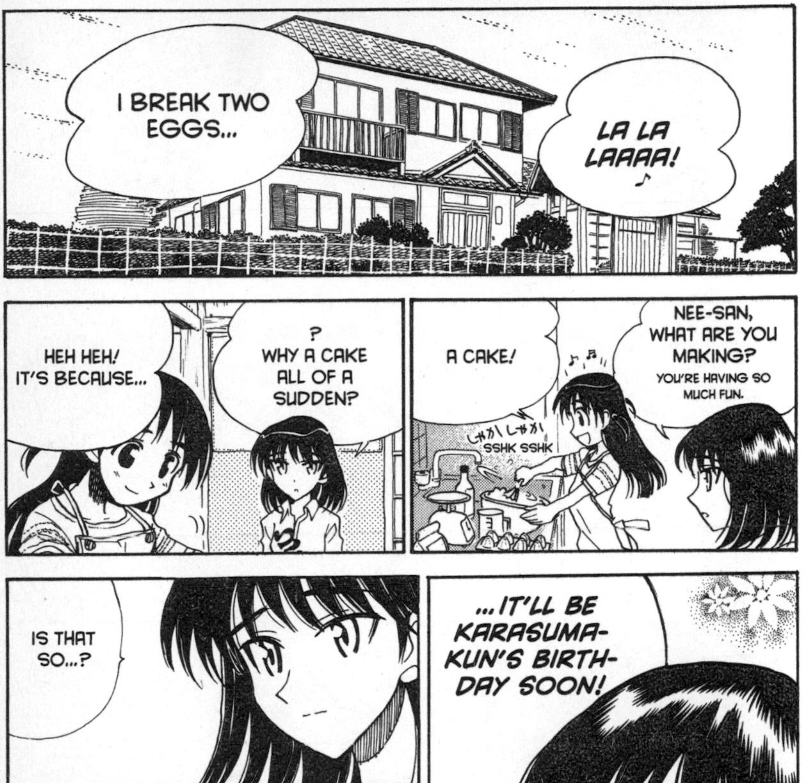
LA LA LAAAA! ♪
I BREAK TWO EGGS...
NEE-SAN, WHAT ARE YOU MAKING? YOU'RE HAVING SO MUCH FUN.
A CAKE!
しゃかしゃか SSHK SSHK
? WHY A CAKE ALL OF A SUDDEN?
HEH HEH! IT'S BECAUSE...
...IT'LL BE KARASUMA-KUN'S BIRTHDAY SOON!
IS THAT SO...?
CAN I HELP?
NO WAY!
I HAVE TO MAKE IT MYSELF FOR IT TO HAVE ANY MEANING.
しゃかしゃか! SSHK SSHK

#98 THE BIRTHDAY PARTY

N-NEE-SAN...
UM...
......
A-ANYWAY, I THINK IT WOULD BE JUST FINE IF YOU BOUGHT KARASUMA-KUN SOMETHING NICE AS A PRESENT.
BUT I HAVE NO IDEA WHAT WOULD MAKE A MAN HAPPY.
BESIDES, KARASUMA-KUN IS A LITTLE ON THE STRANGE SIDE...
N-NEE-SAN...
AH! HELLO...?
SORRY FOR THE SUDDEN CALL. YAKUMO GAVE ME YOUR NUMBER...
TOMORROW...
...I NEED YOU TO COME SHOPPING WITH ME.

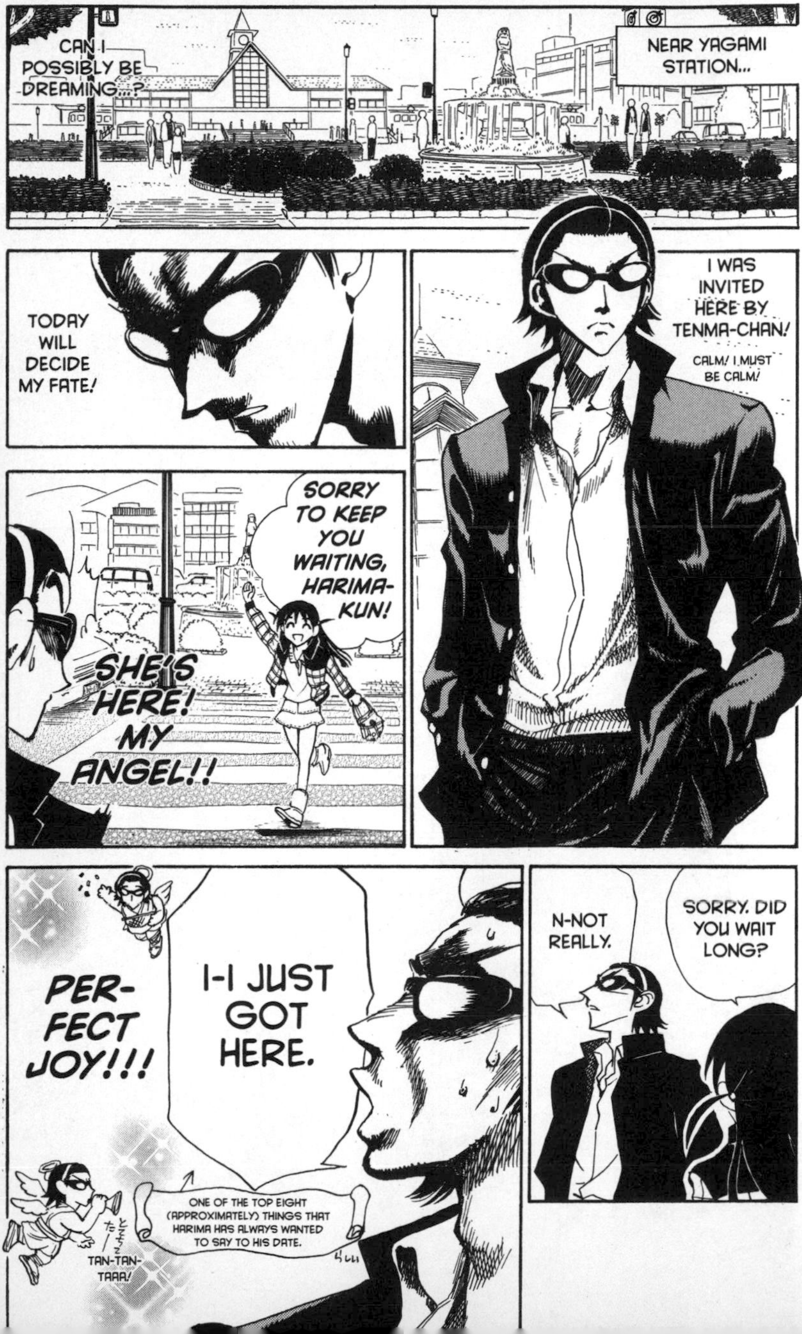
NEAR YAGAMI STATION...
CAN I POSSIBLY BE DREAMING...?
I WAS INVITED HERE BY TENMA-CHAN!
CALM! I MUST BE CALM!
TODAY WILL DECIDE MY FATE!
SORRY TO KEEP YOU WAITING, HARIMA-KUN!
SHE'S HERE! MY ANGEL!!
SORRY. DID YOU WAIT LONG?
N-NOT REALLY.
I-I JUST GOT HERE.
PER-FECT JOY!!!
ONE OF THE TOP EIGHT (APPROXIMATELY) THINGS THAT HARIMA HAS ALWAYS WANTED TO SAY TO HIS DATE.
TAN-TAN-TAAA!

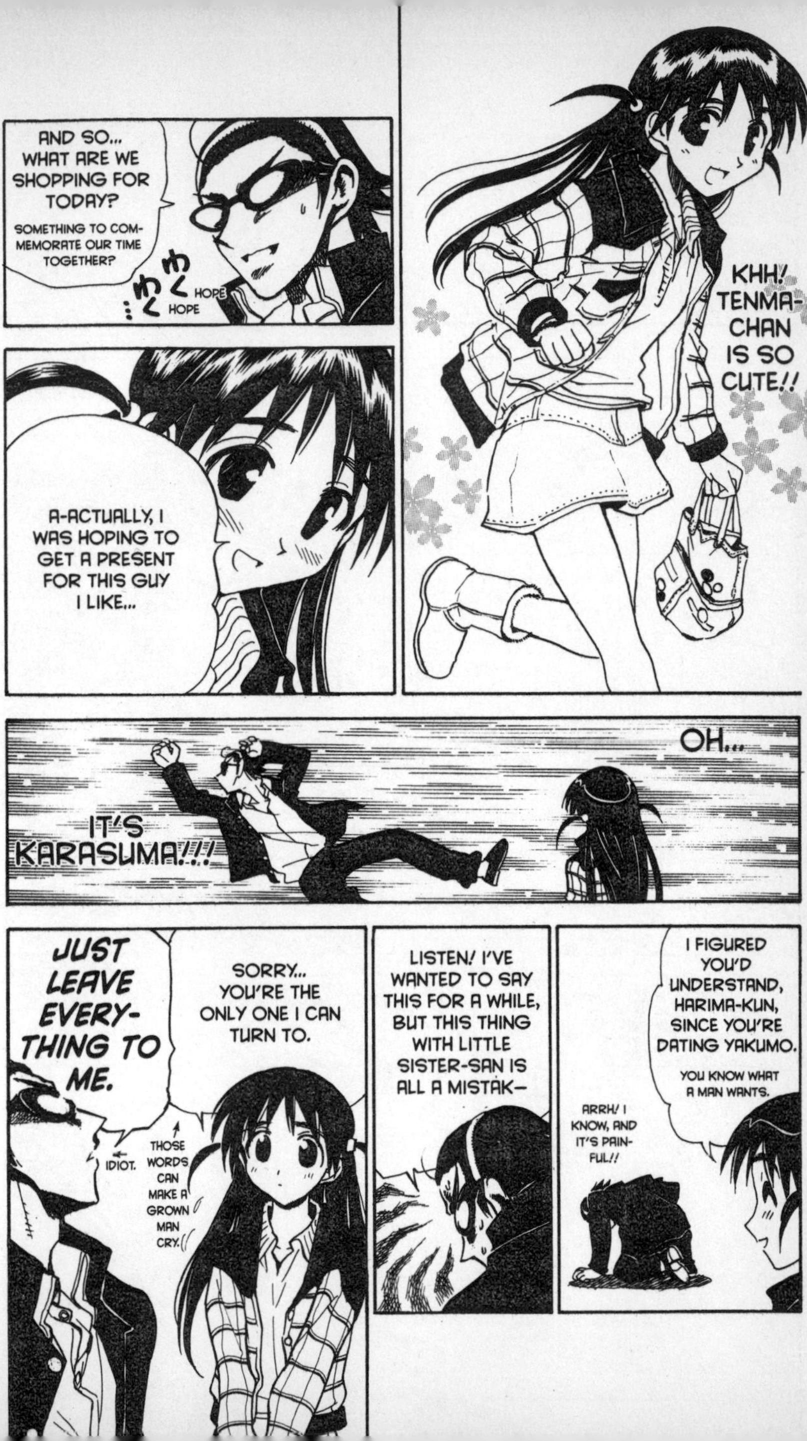
KHH! TENMA-CHAN IS SO CUTE!!
AND SO... WHAT ARE WE SHOPPING FOR TODAY?
SOMETHING TO COM-MEMORATE OUR TIME TOGETHER?
HOPE HOPE
A-ACTUALLY, I WAS HOPING TO GET A PRESENT FOR THIS GUY I LIKE...
OH...
IT'S KARASUMA!!!
I FIGURED YOU'D UNDERSTAND, HARIMA-KUN, SINCE YOU'RE DATING YAKUMO.
YOU KNOW WHAT A MAN WANTS.
ARRH! I KNOW, AND IT'S PAIN-FUL!!
LISTEN! I'VE WANTED TO SAY THIS FOR A WHILE, BUT THIS THING WITH LITTLE SISTER-SAN IS ALL A MISTAK—
SORRY... YOU'RE THE ONLY ONE I CAN TURN TO.
JUST LEAVE EVERY-THING TO ME.
THOSE WORDS CAN MAKE A GROWN MAN CRY.
IDIOT.

Tenma: Loves Karasuma-kun. In Case You Didn't Know.

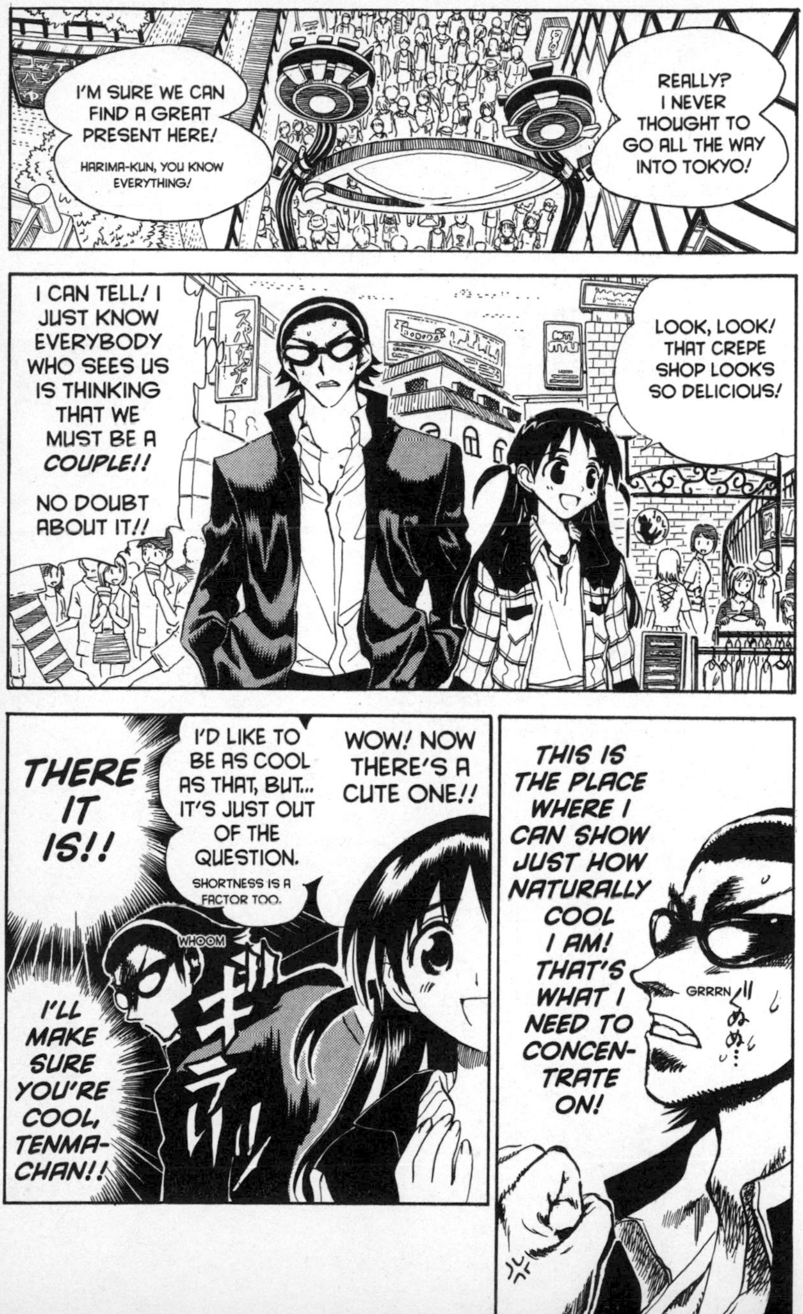
REALLY? I NEVER THOUGHT TO GO ALL THE WAY INTO TOKYO!
I'M SURE WE CAN FIND A GREAT PRESENT HERE!
HARIMA-KUN, YOU KNOW EVERYTHING!
LOOK, LOOK! THAT CREPE SHOP LOOKS SO DELICIOUS!
I CAN TELL! I JUST KNOW EVERYBODY WHO SEES US IS THINKING THAT WE MUST BE A COUPLE!!
NO DOUBT ABOUT IT!!
THIS IS THE PLACE WHERE I CAN SHOW JUST HOW NATURALLY COOL I AM! THAT'S WHAT I NEED TO CONCEN-TRATE ON!
GRRRN
WOW! NOW THERE'S A CUTE ONE!!
I'D LIKE TO BE AS COOL AS THAT, BUT... IT'S JUST OUT OF THE QUESTION.
SHORTNESS IS A FACTOR TOO.
THERE IT IS!!
WHOOM
I'LL MAKE SURE YOU'RE COOL, TENMA-CHAN!!

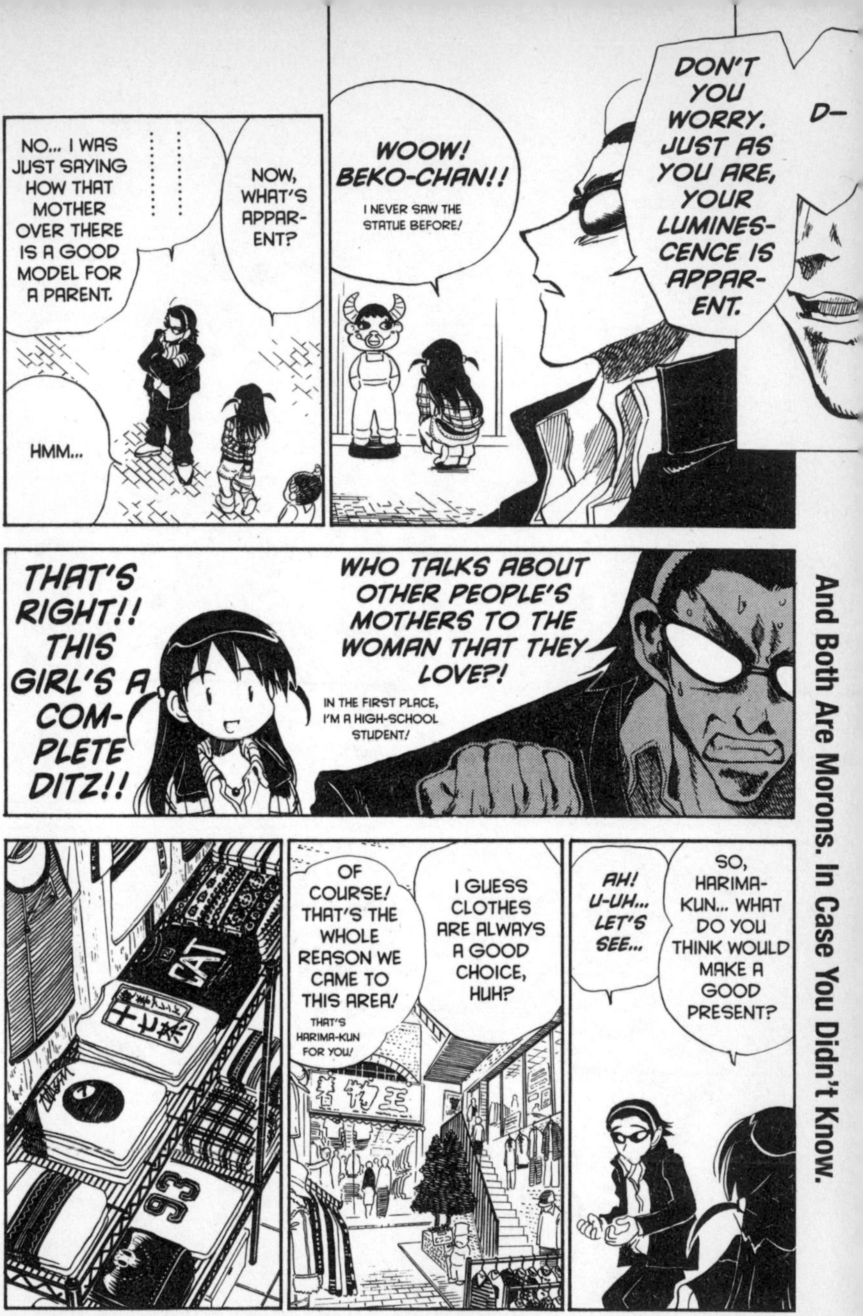
DON'T YOU WORRY. JUST AS YOU ARE, YOUR LUMINESCENCE IS APPARENT.
D—
WOOW! BEKO-CHAN!!
I NEVER SAW THE STATUE BEFORE!
......
NOW, WHAT'S APPARENT?
NO... I WAS JUST SAYING HOW THAT MOTHER OVER THERE IS A GOOD MODEL FOR A PARENT.
HMM...
WHO TALKS ABOUT OTHER PEOPLE'S MOTHERS TO THE WOMAN THAT THEY LOVE?!
IN THE FIRST PLACE, I'M A HIGH-SCHOOL STUDENT!
THAT'S RIGHT!! THIS GIRL'S A COMPLETE DITZ!!
SO, HARIMA-KUN... WHAT DO YOU THINK WOULD MAKE A GOOD PRESENT?
AH! U-UH... LET'S SEE...
I GUESS CLOTHES ARE ALWAYS A GOOD CHOICE, HUH?
OF COURSE! THAT'S THE WHOLE REASON WE CAME TO THIS AREA!
THAT'S HARIMA-KUN FOR YOU!
CAT

And Both Are Morons. In Case You Didn't Know.

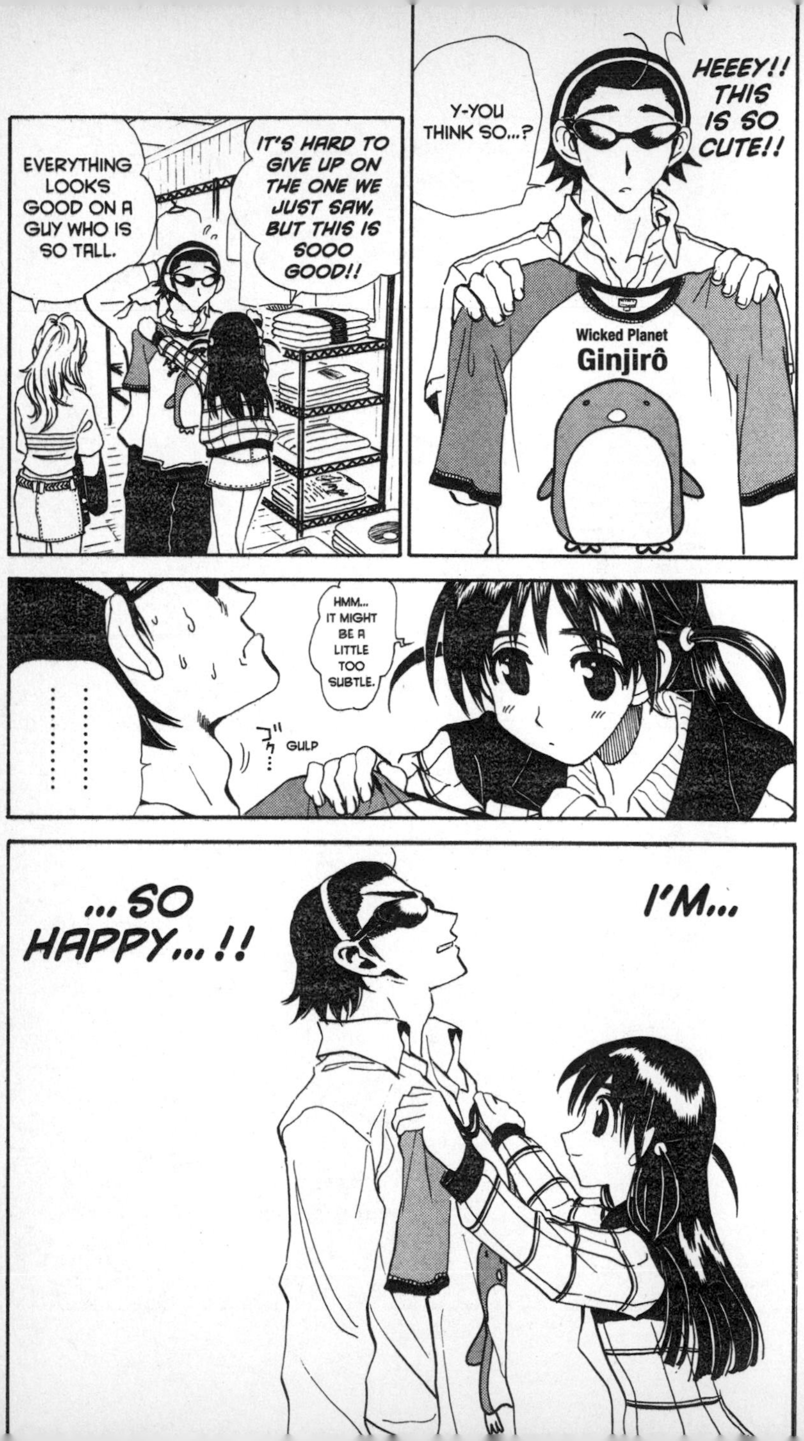
HEEEY!! THIS IS SO CUTE!!
Y-YOU THINK SO...?
Wicked Planet Ginjirô
IT'S HARD TO GIVE UP ON THE ONE WE JUST SAW, BUT THIS IS SOOO GOOD!!
EVERYTHING LOOKS GOOD ON A GUY WHO IS SO TALL.
HMM... IT MIGHT BE A LITTLE TOO SUBTLE.
GULP
......
......
I'M...
...SO HAPPY...!!

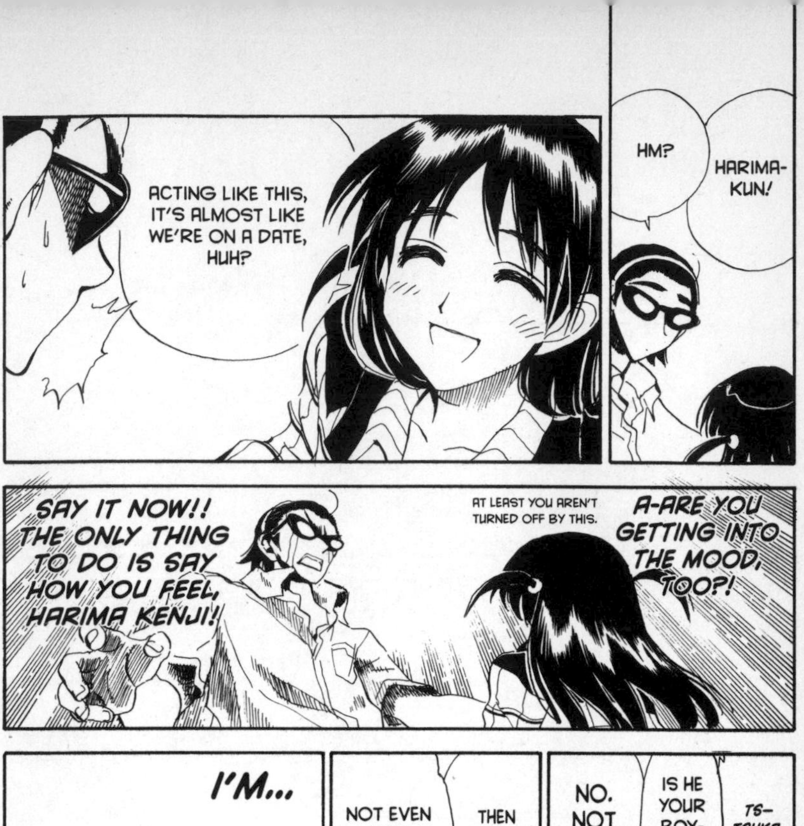
HARIMA-KUN!
HM?
ACTING LIKE THIS, IT'S ALMOST LIKE WE'RE ON A DATE, HUH?
A-ARE YOU GETTING INTO THE MOOD, TOO?!
AT LEAST YOU AREN'T TURNED OFF BY THIS.
SAY IT NOW!! THE ONLY THING TO DO IS SAY HOW YOU FEEL, HARIMA KENJI!
TS-TSUKA-MOTO!! ACTU-ALLY...!!
IS HE YOUR BOY-FRIEND?
HE'S A PRETTY COOL GUY.
NO. NOT EVEN CLOSE.
THEN YOU'RE JUST FRIENDS?
NOT EVEN THAT. HE'S MY SISTER'S BOY-FRIEND.
I'M...
...SO UNHAPPY...!!

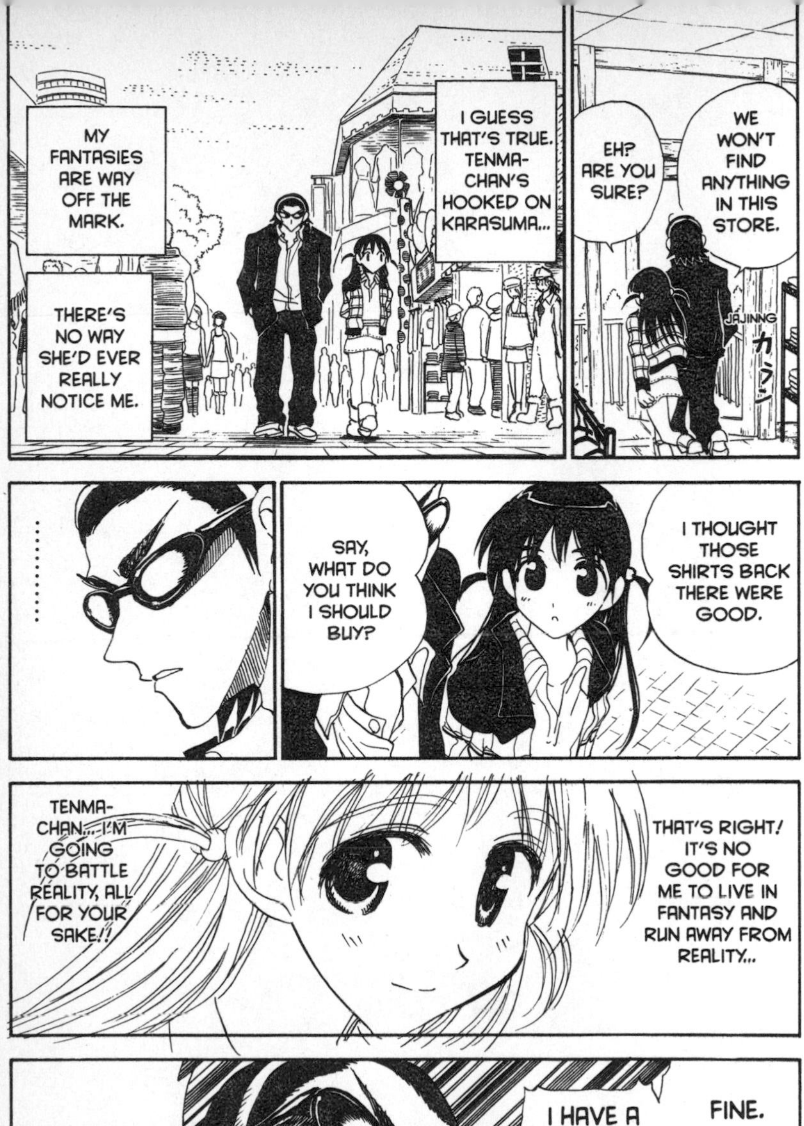
WE WON'T FIND ANYTHING IN THIS STORE.
EH? ARE YOU SURE?
JAJINNG
I GUESS THAT'S TRUE. TENMA-CHAN'S HOOKED ON KARASUMA...
MY FANTASIES ARE WAY OFF THE MARK.
THERE'S NO WAY SHE'D EVER REALLY NOTICE ME.
I THOUGHT THOSE SHIRTS BACK THERE WERE GOOD.
SAY, WHAT DO YOU THINK I SHOULD BUY?
....
THAT'S RIGHT! IT'S NO GOOD FOR ME TO LIVE IN FANTASY AND RUN AWAY FROM REALITY...
TENMA-CHAN... I'M GOING TO BATTLE REALITY, ALL FOR YOUR SAKE!!
FINE. I'LL TELL YOU!!
I HAVE A SPECIAL PRESENT CHOSEN ESPECIALLY FOR YOU!!
OBSERVE!!

Who Needs That...?

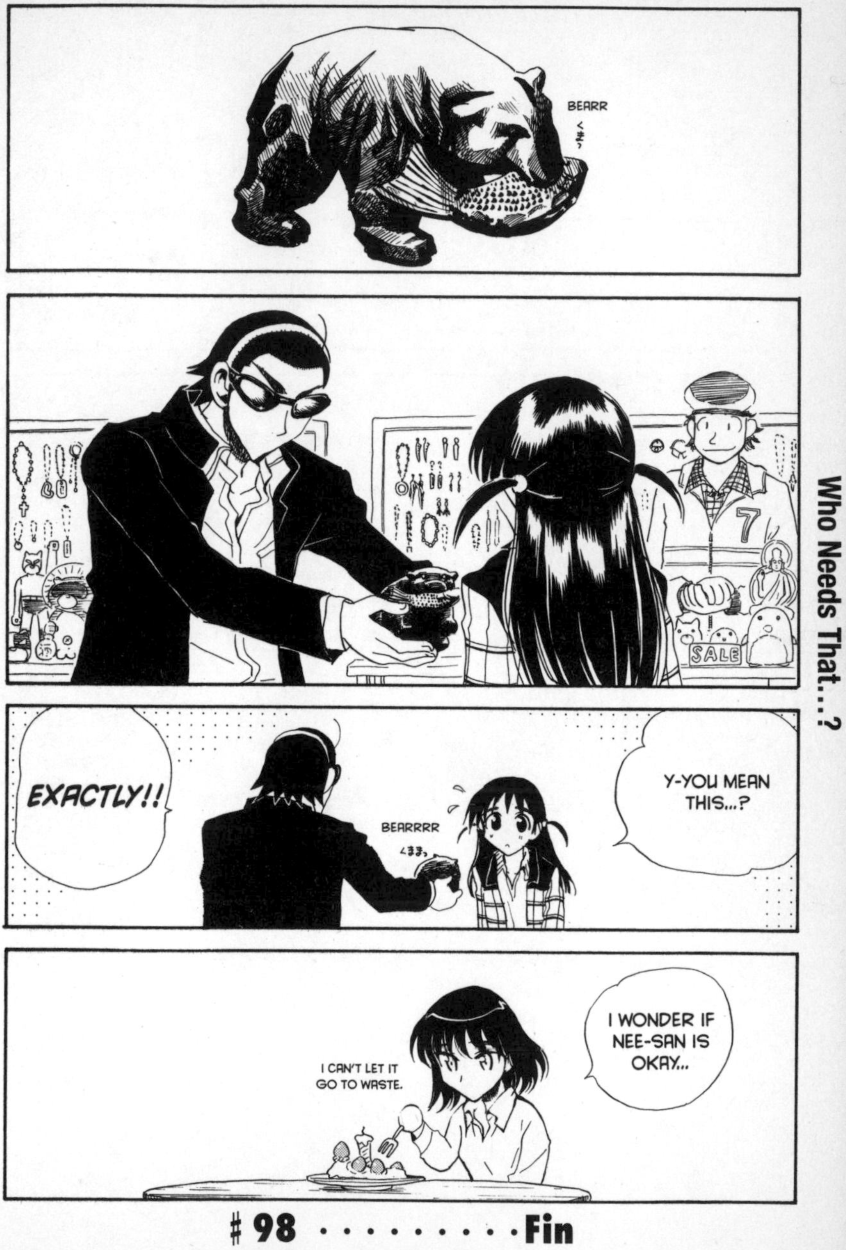
BEARR
くまっ
Y-YOU MEAN THIS...?
BEARRRR
くままっ
EXACTLY!!
I WONDER IF NEE-SAN IS OKAY...
I CAN'T LET IT GO TO WASTE.

98 ....Fin

99 THE TRUE HEARTED

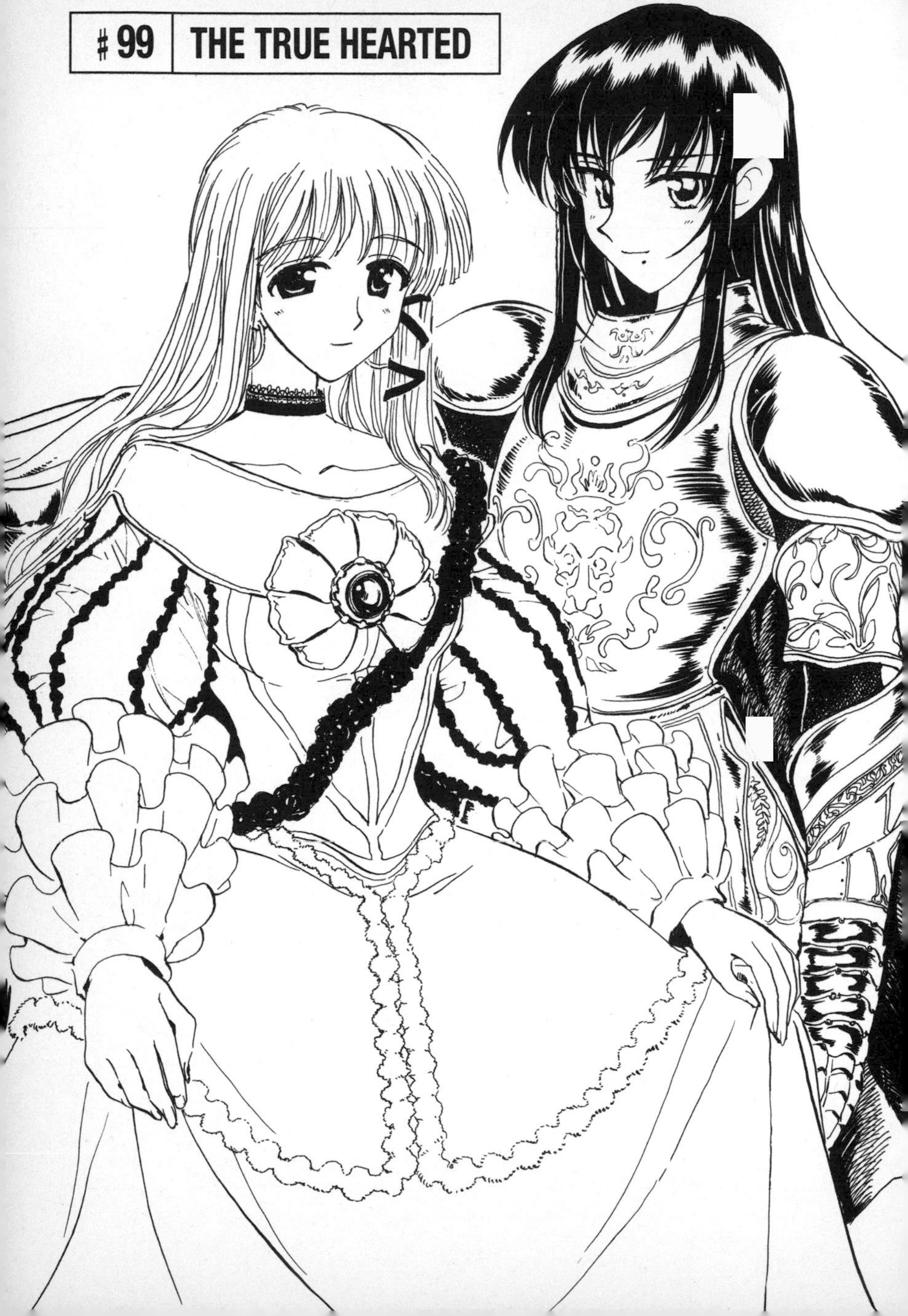

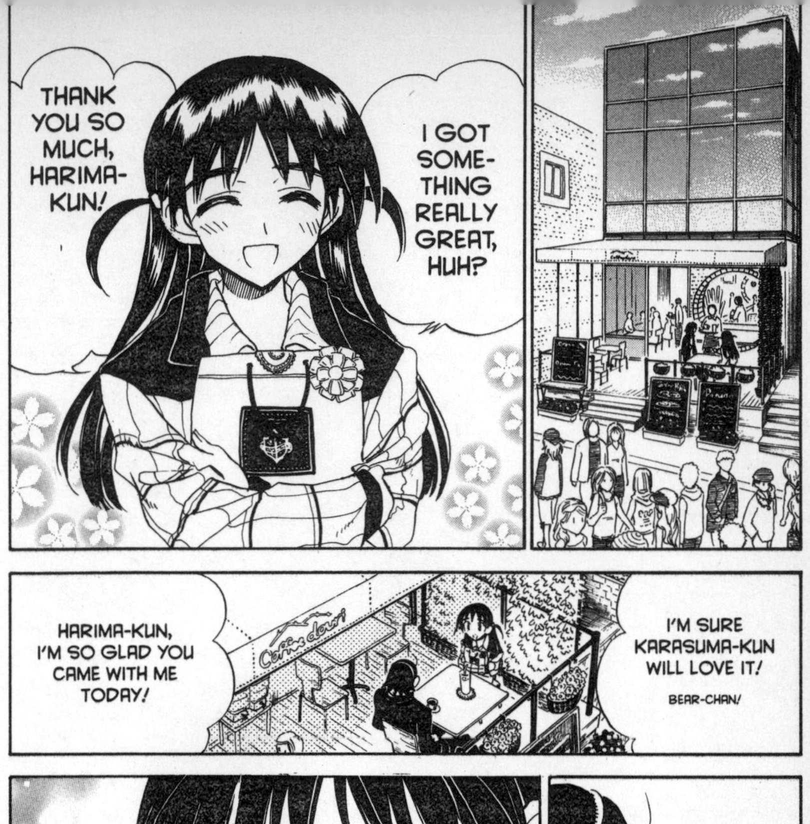
I GOT SOMETHING REALLY GREAT, HUH?
THANK YOU SO MUCH, HARIMA-KUN!
I'M SURE KARASUMA-KUN WILL LOVE IT!
BEAR-CHAN!
HARIMA-KUN, I'M SO GLAD YOU CAME WITH ME TODAY!
SORRY, TENMA-CHAN! I DOUBT ANYBODY WOULD BE HAPPY RECEIVING THAT GIFT.
BUT IF I DIDN'T RELEASE THE DEVIL INSIDE ME, I'D NEVER GET MY CHANCE WITH YOU...
ズキ
ZHAAN

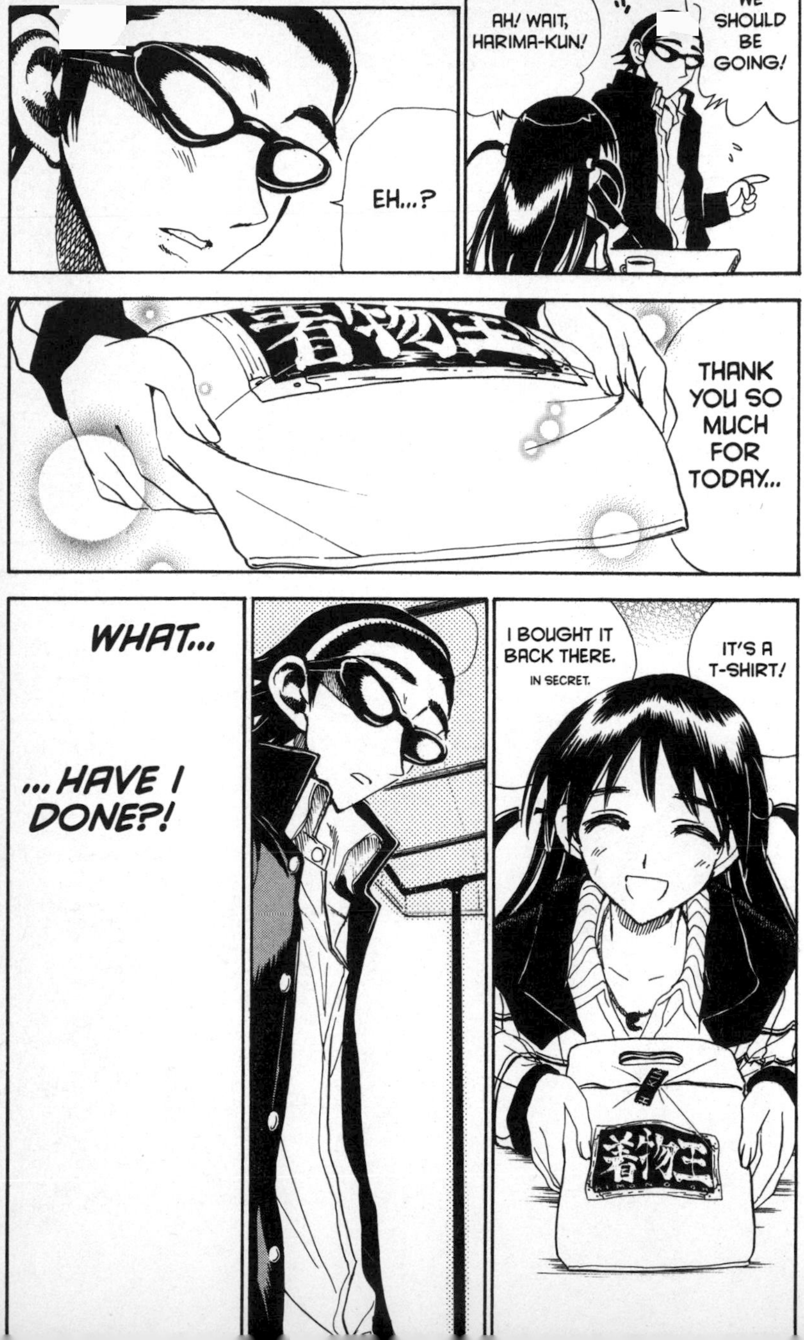
TH-THEN WE SHOULD BE GOING!
SKRRT
AH! WAIT, HARIMA-KUN!
EH...?
THANK YOU SO MUCH FOR TODAY...
IT'S A T-SHIRT!
I BOUGHT IT BACK THERE.
IN SECRET.
WHAT...
...HAVE I DONE?!

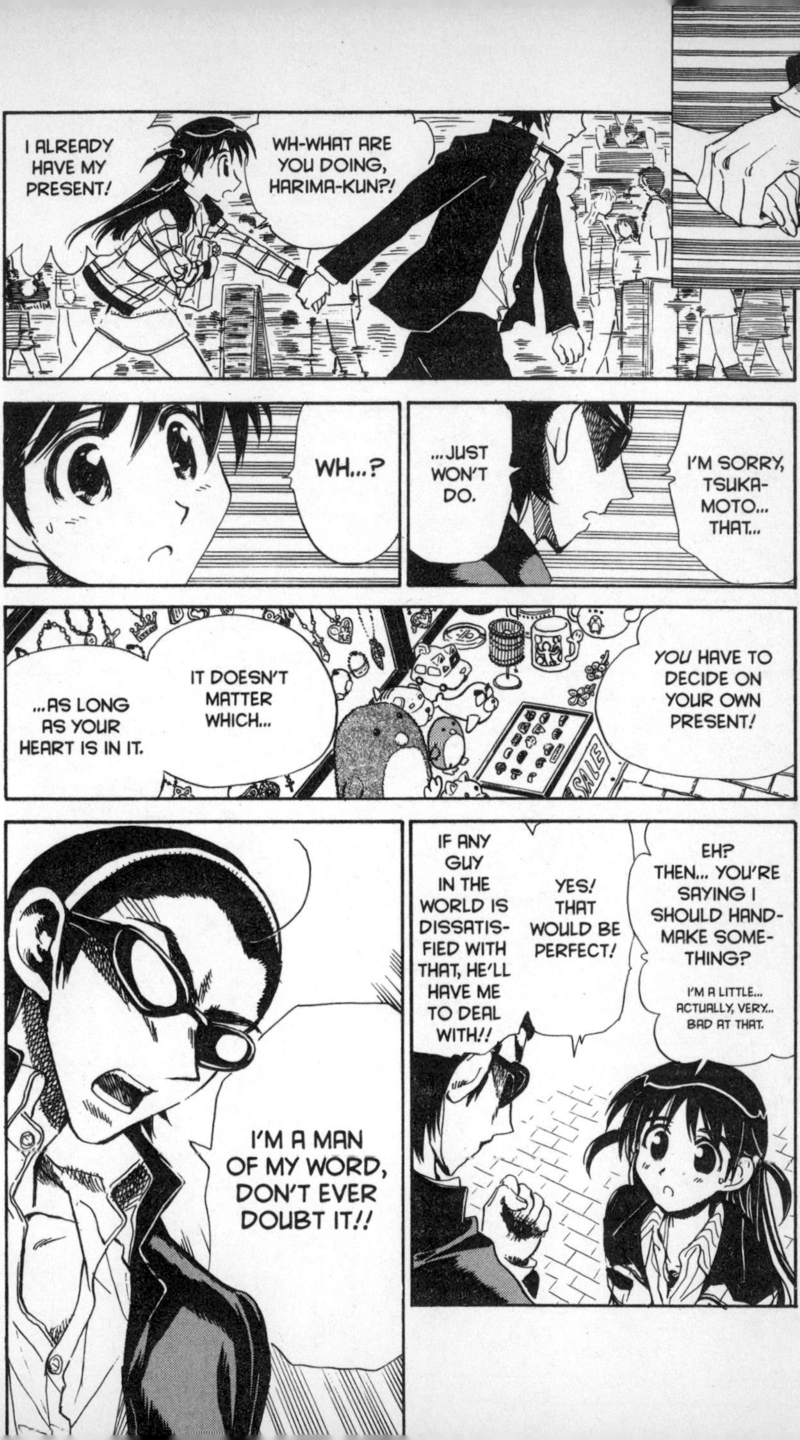
WH-WHAT ARE YOU DOING, HARIMA-KUN?!
I ALREADY HAVE MY PRESENT!
I'M SORRY, TSUKAMOTO... THAT...
...JUST WON'T DO.
WH...?
YOU HAVE TO DECIDE ON YOUR OWN PRESENT!
IT DOESN'T MATTER WHICH...
...AS LONG AS YOUR HEART IS IN IT.
EH? THEN... YOU'RE SAYING I SHOULD HAND-MAKE SOMETHING?
I'M A LITTLE... ACTUALLY, VERY... BAD AT THAT.
YES! THAT WOULD BE PERFECT!
IF ANY GUY IN THE WORLD IS DISSATISFIED WITH THAT, HE'LL HAVE ME TO DEAL WITH!!
I'M A MAN OF MY WORD, DON'T EVER DOUBT IT!!

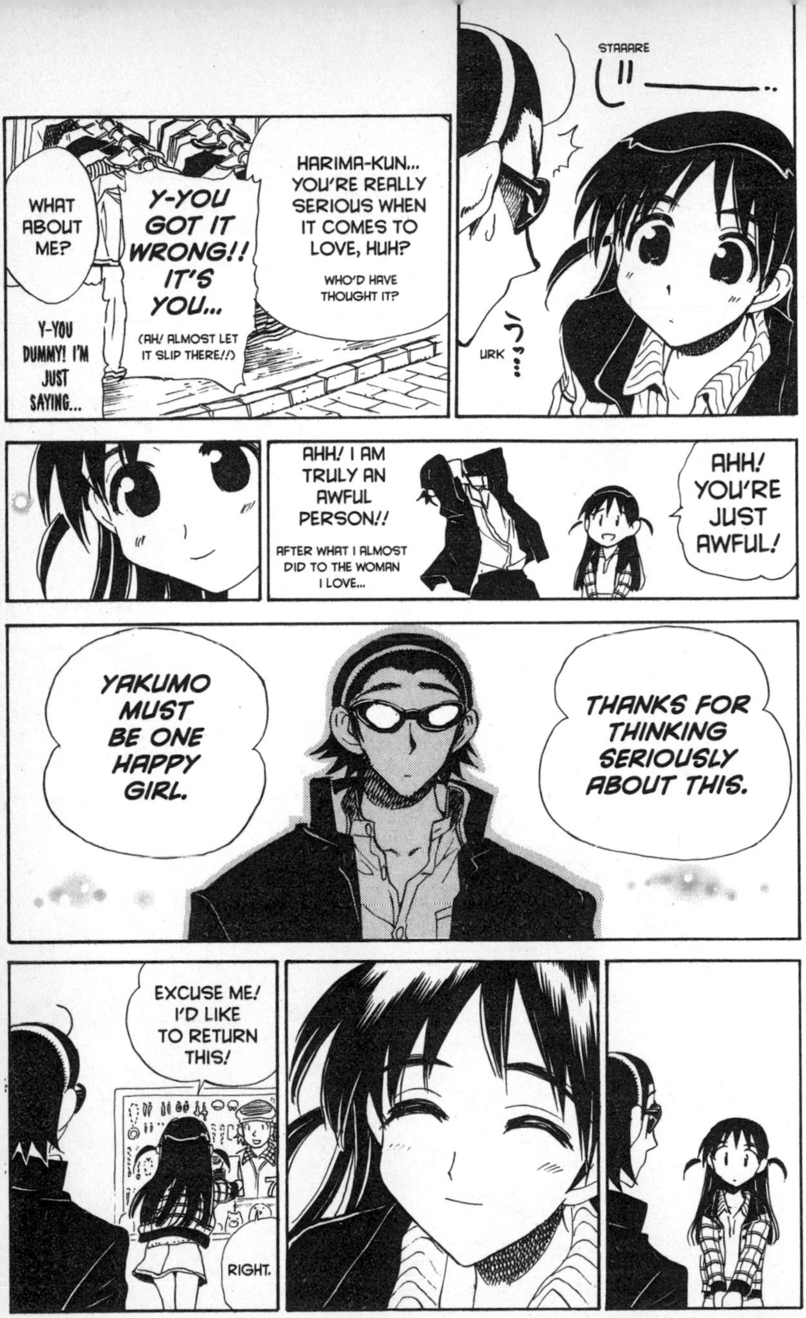
STAAARE
URK
HARIMA-KUN... YOU'RE REALLY SERIOUS WHEN IT COMES TO LOVE, HUH?
WHO'D HAVE THOUGHT IT?
Y-YOU GOT IT WRONG!! IT'S YOU...
(AH! ALMOST LET IT SLIP THERE!!)
WHAT ABOUT ME?
Y-YOU DUMMY! I'M JUST SAYING...
AHH! YOU'RE JUST AWFUL!
AHH! I AM TRULY AN AWFUL PERSON!!
AFTER WHAT I ALMOST DID TO THE WOMAN I LOVE...
THANKS FOR THINKING SERIOUSLY ABOUT THIS.
YAKUMO MUST BE ONE HAPPY GIRL.
EXCUSE ME! I'D LIKE TO RETURN THIS!
RIGHT.

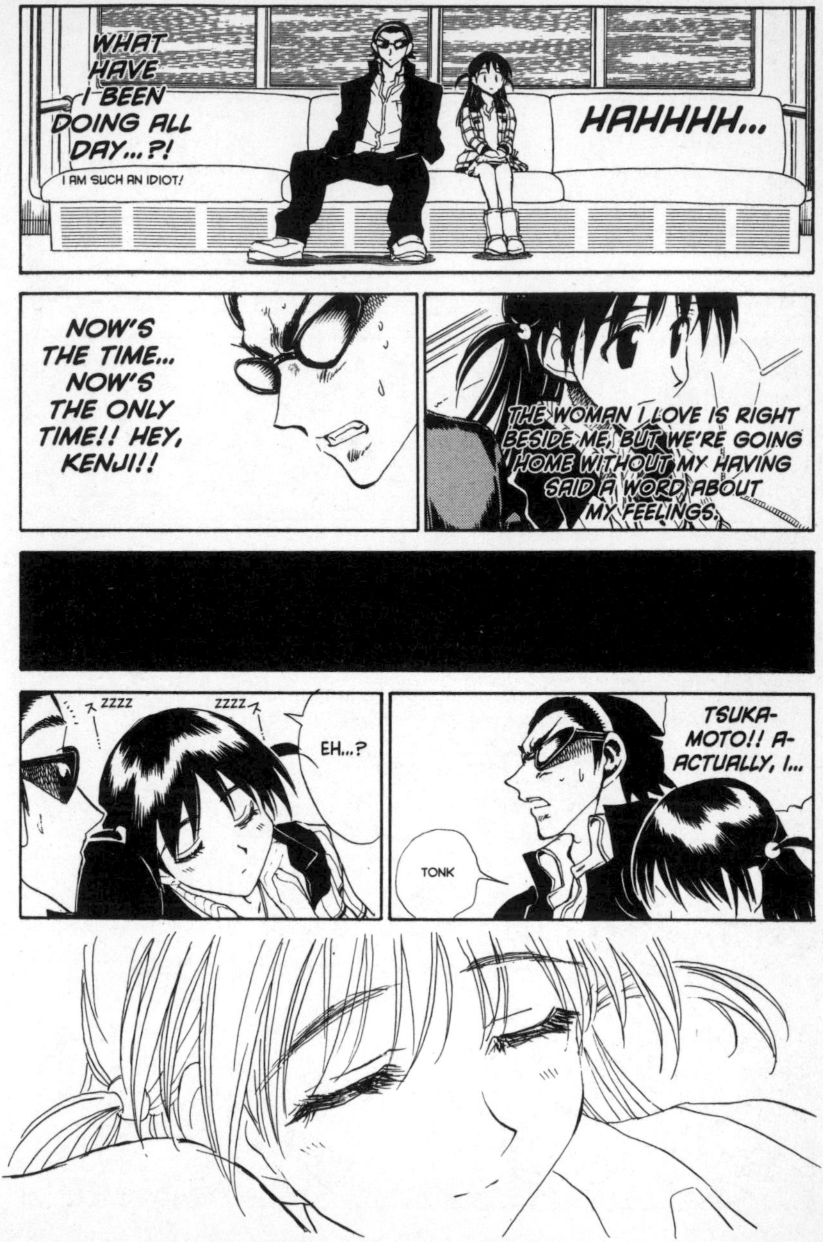
HAHHHH...
WHAT HAVE I BEEN DOING ALL DAY...?!
I AM SUCH AN IDIOT!
THE WOMAN I LOVE IS RIGHT BESIDE ME, BUT WE'RE GOING HOME WITHOUT MY HAVING SAID A WORD ABOUT MY FEELINGS.
NOW'S THE TIME... NOW'S THE ONLY TIME!! HEY, KENJI!!
TSUKA-MOTO!! A-ACTUALLY, I...
TONK
EH...?
ZZZZ
ZZZZ

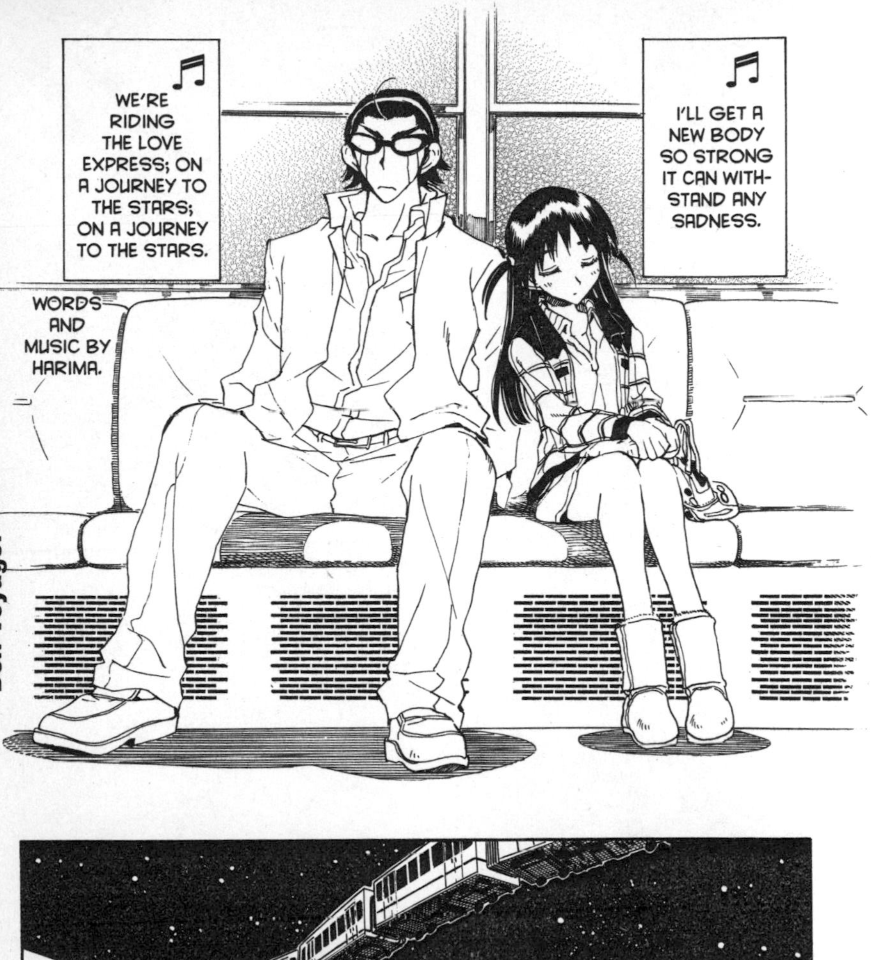
I'LL GET A NEW BODY SO STRONG IT CAN WITH-STAND ANY SADNESS.
WE'RE RIDING THE LOVE EXPRESS; ON A JOURNEY TO THE STARS; ON A JOURNEY TO THE STARS.
WORDS AND MUSIC BY HARIMA.

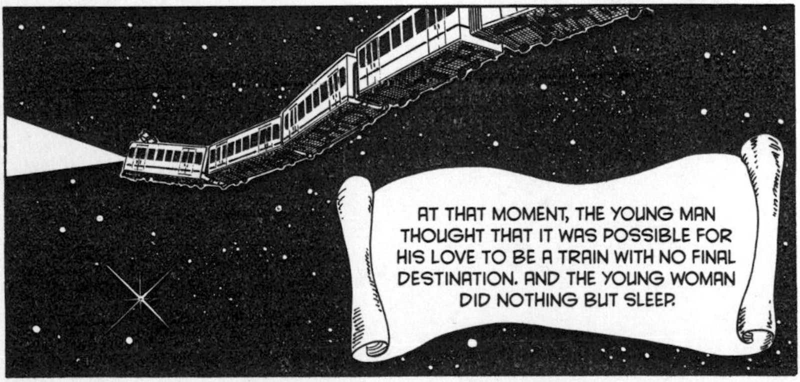
AT THAT MOMENT, THE YOUNG MAN THOUGHT THAT IT WAS POSSIBLE FOR HIS LOVE TO BE A TRAIN WITH NO FINAL DESTINATION. AND THE YOUNG WOMAN DID NOTHING BUT SLEEP.

 # 99 ·········Fin

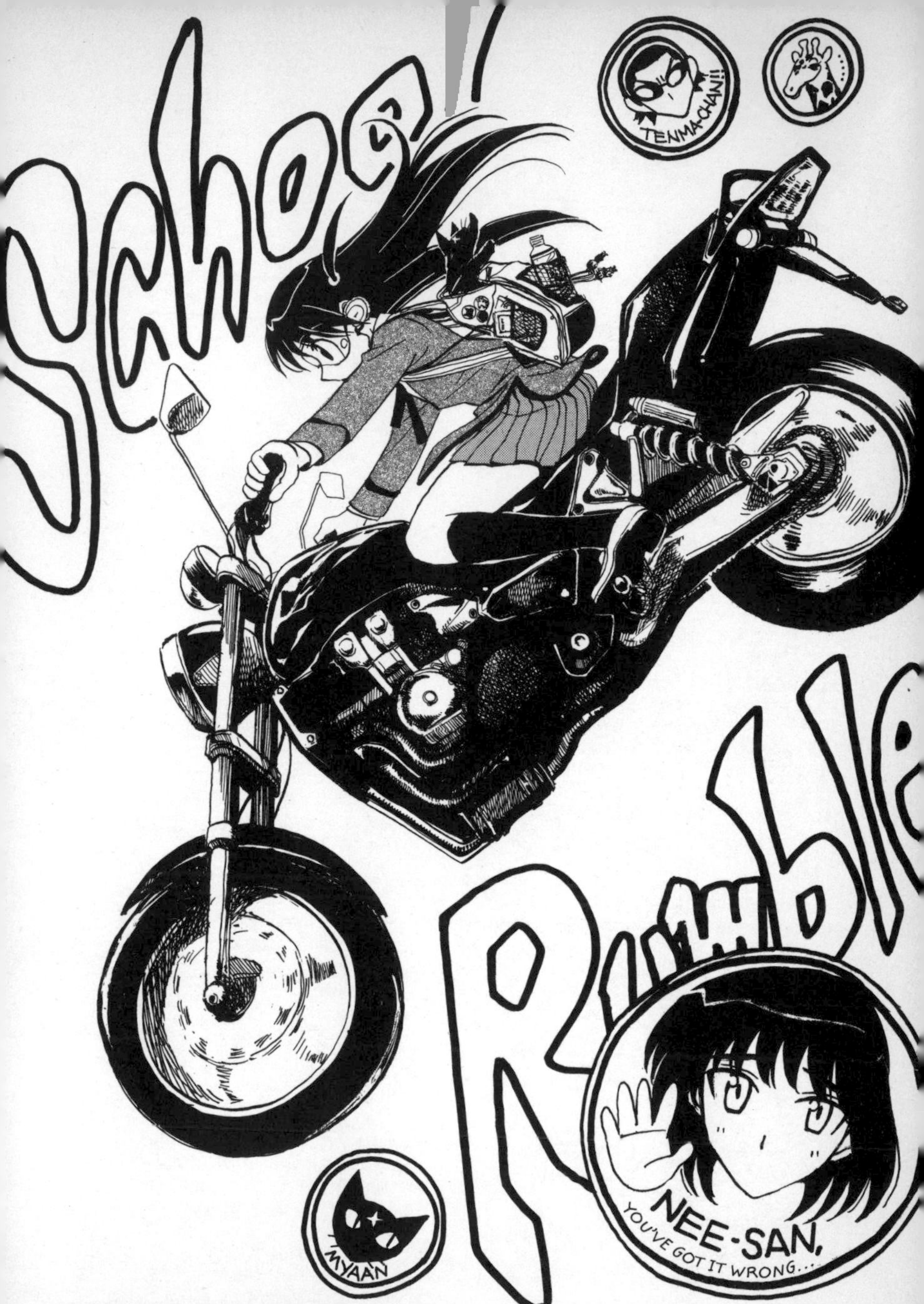
School Rumble
TENMA-CHAN!!
NEE-SAN, YOU'VE GOT IT WRONG...
MYAAN

# 100	GELOSIA

Sawachika Eri: Bad at Japanese Language-Based Subjects. Spent Too Much Time Overseas.

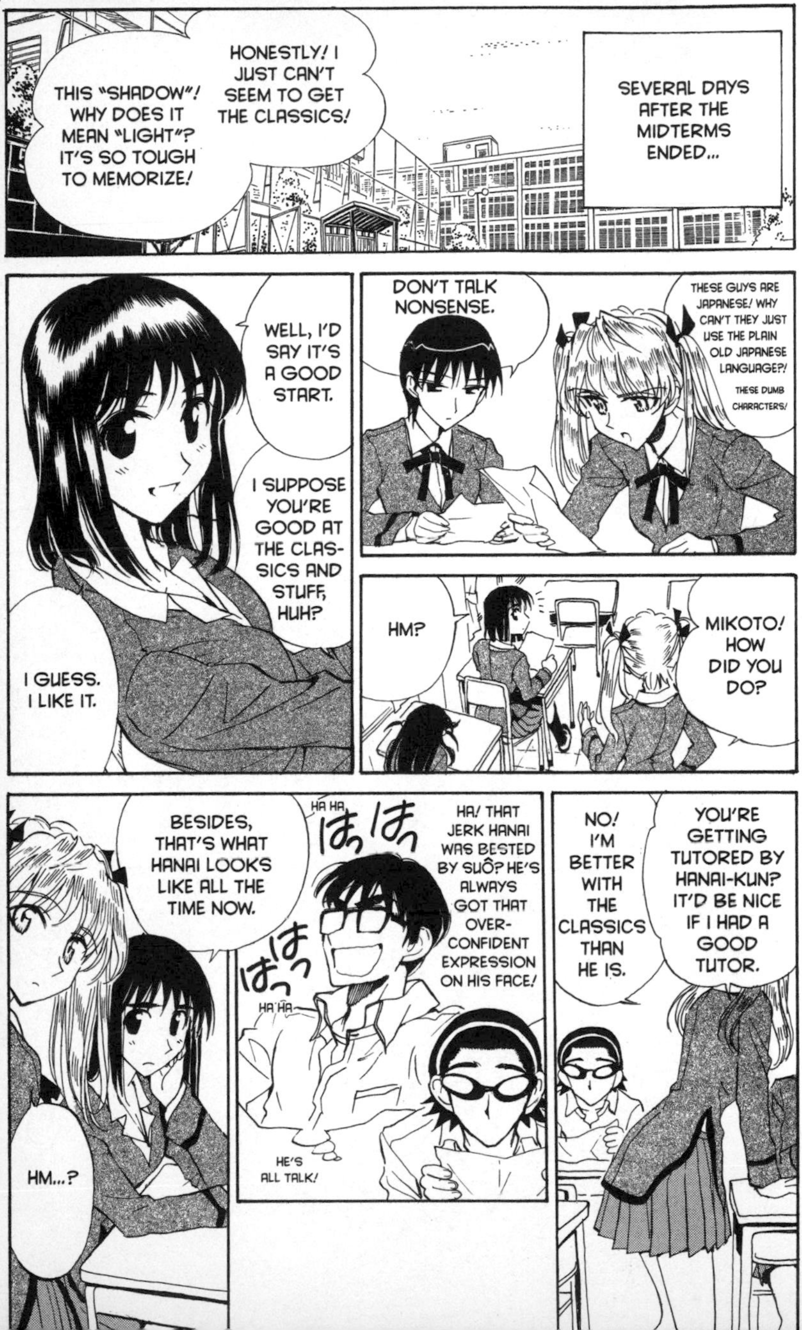
SEVERAL DAYS AFTER THE MIDTERMS ENDED...
HONESTLY! I JUST CAN'T SEEM TO GET THE CLASSICS!
THIS "SHADOW"! WHY DOES IT MEAN "LIGHT"? IT'S SO TOUGH TO MEMORIZE!
THESE GUYS ARE JAPANESE! WHY CAN'T THEY JUST USE THE PLAIN OLD JAPANESE LANGUAGE?!
THESE DUMB CHARACTERS!
DON'T TALK NONSENSE.
MIKOTO! HOW DID YOU DO?
HM?
WELL, I'D SAY IT'S A GOOD START.
I SUPPOSE YOU'RE GOOD AT THE CLASSICS AND STUFF, HUH?
I GUESS. I LIKE IT.
YOU'RE GETTING TUTORED BY HANAI-KUN? IT'D BE NICE IF I HAD A GOOD TUTOR.
NO! I'M BETTER WITH THE CLASSICS THAN HE IS.
HA! THAT JERK HANAI WAS BESTED BY SUÔ? HE'S ALWAYS GOT THAT OVER-CONFIDENT EXPRESSION ON HIS FACE!
HA HA
はっはっ
はっはっ
HA HA
HE'S ALL TALK!
BESIDES, THAT'S WHAT HANAI LOOKS LIKE ALL THE TIME NOW.
HM...?

Hanai Haruki: Stench of Death.

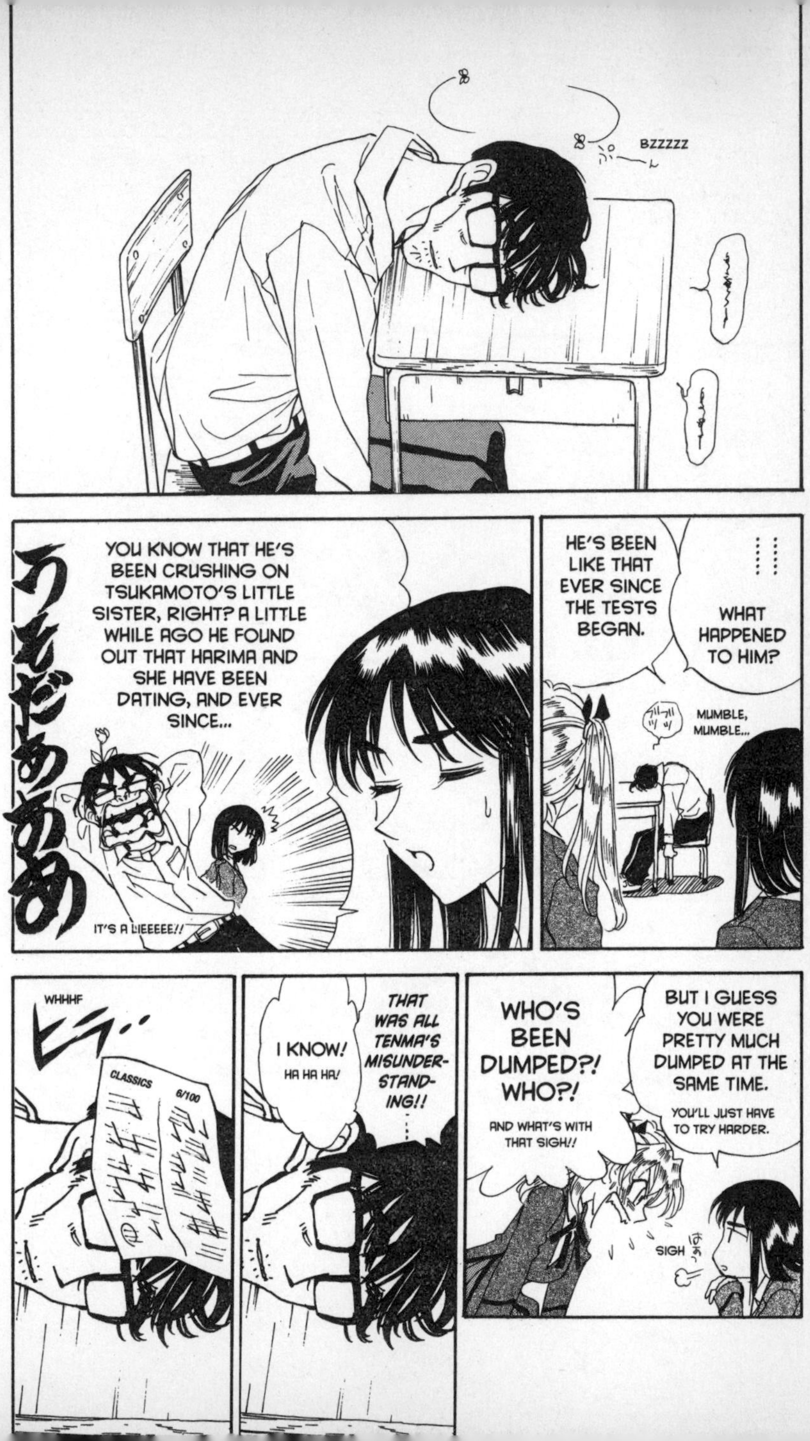
BZZZZZ
......
WHAT HAPPENED TO HIM?
HE'S BEEN LIKE THAT EVER SINCE THE TESTS BEGAN.
MUMBLE, MUMBLE...
YOU KNOW THAT HE'S BEEN CRUSHING ON TSUKAMOTO'S LITTLE SISTER, RIGHT? A LITTLE WHILE AGO HE FOUND OUT THAT HARIMA AND SHE HAVE BEEN DATING, AND EVER SINCE...
IT'S A LIEEEEE!!
BUT I GUESS YOU WERE PRETTY MUCH DUMPED AT THE SAME TIME.
YOU'LL JUST HAVE TO TRY HARDER.
SIGH
WHO'S BEEN DUMPED?! WHO?!
AND WHAT'S WITH THAT SIGH!!
THAT WAS ALL TENMA'S MISUNDER-STAND-ING!!
I KNOW!
HA HA HA!
...
WHHHF
CLASSICS 6/100

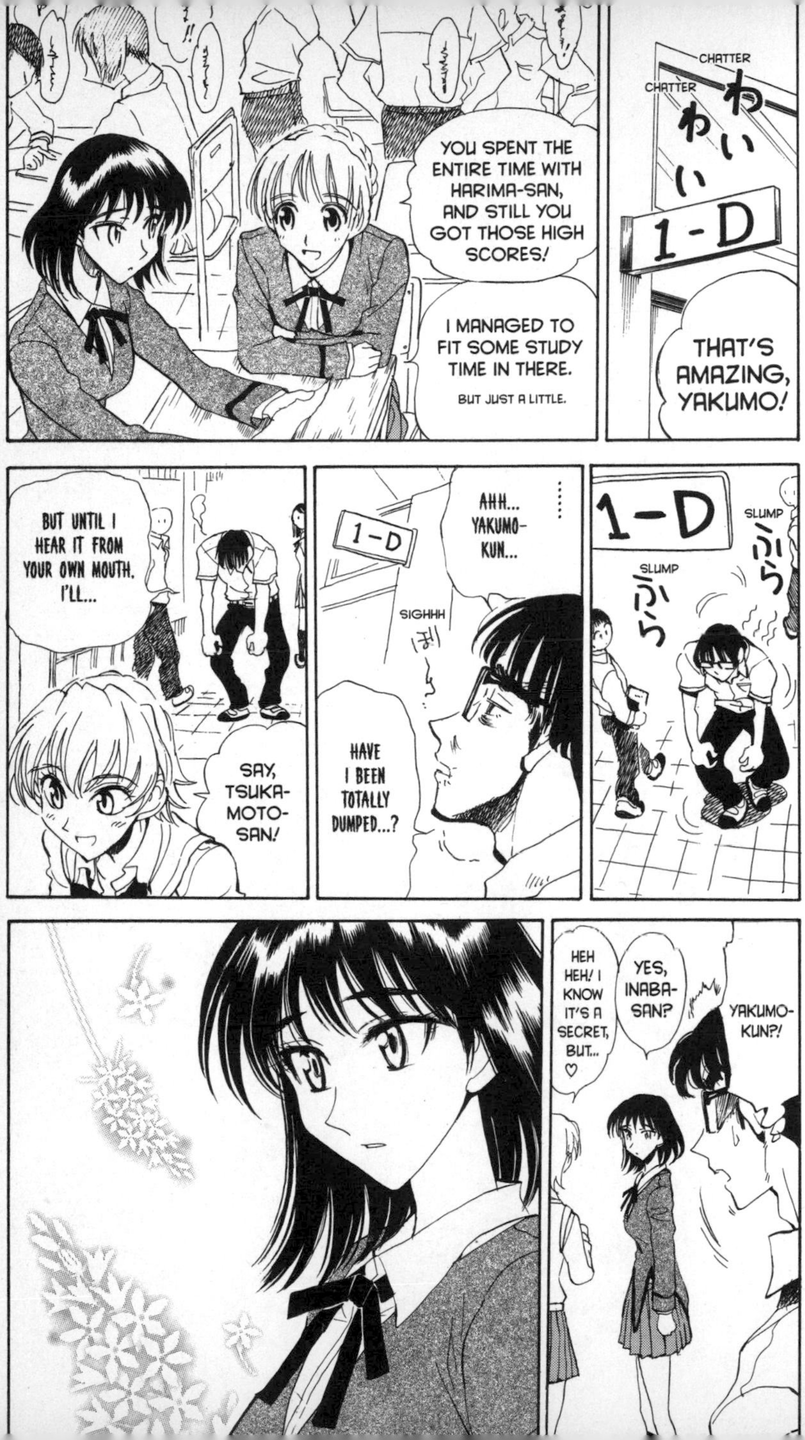
CHATTER
CHATTER
わいわい
1-D
THAT'S AMAZING, YAKUMO!
YOU SPENT THE ENTIRE TIME WITH HARIMA-SAN, AND STILL YOU GOT THOSE HIGH SCORES!
I MANAGED TO FIT SOME STUDY TIME IN THERE.
BUT JUST A LITTLE.
1-D
SLUMP
ふら
SLUMP
ふら
1-D
AHH... YAKUMO-KUN...
......
SIGHHH
HAVE I BEEN TOTALLY DUMPED...?
BUT UNTIL I HEAR IT FROM YOUR OWN MOUTH, I'LL...
SAY, TSUKA-MOTO-SAN!
YAKUMO-KUN?!
YES, INABA-SAN?
HEH HEH! I KNOW IT'S A SECRET, BUT... ♡

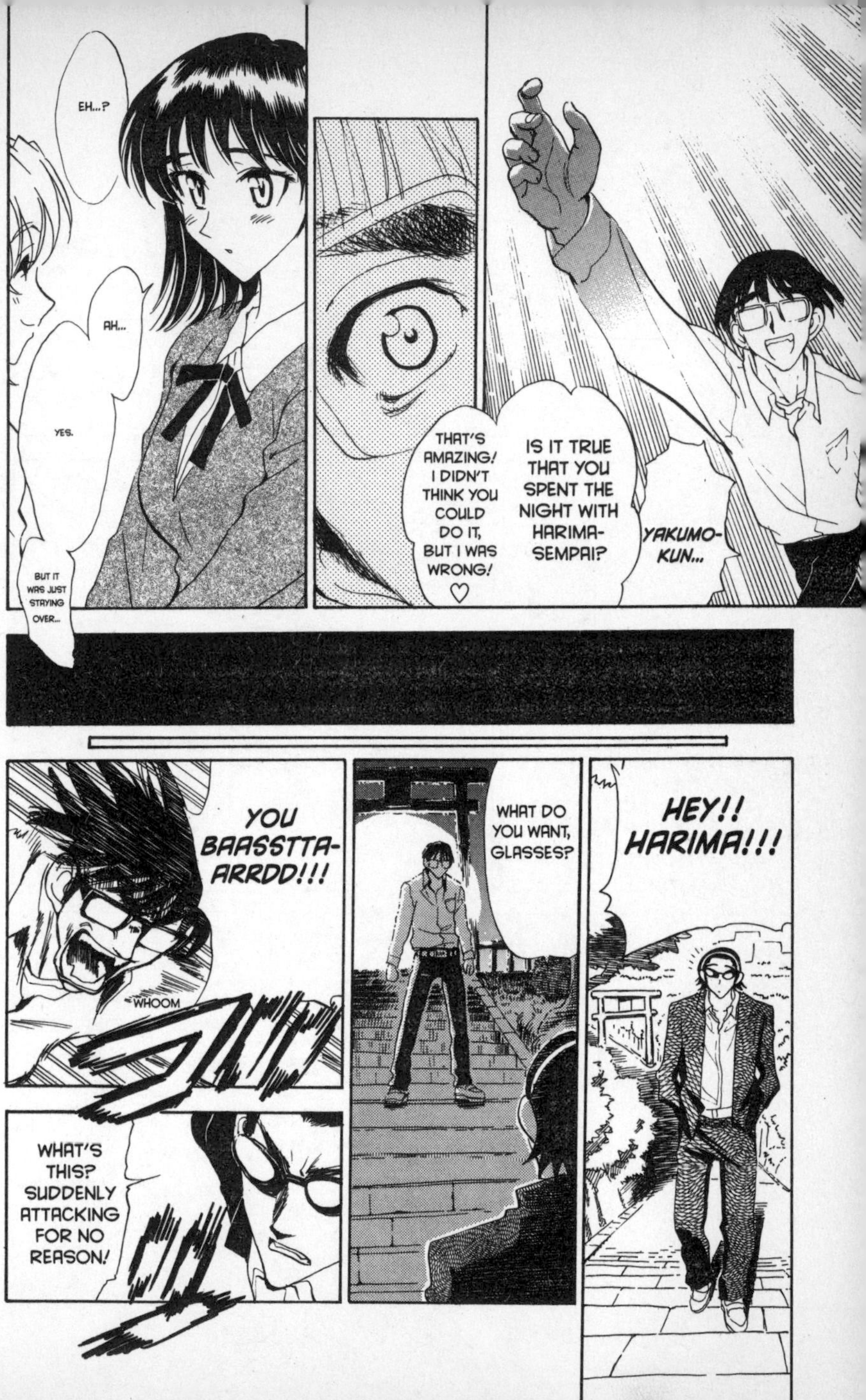
YAKUMO-KUN...
IS IT TRUE THAT YOU SPENT THE NIGHT WITH HARIMA-SEMPAI?
THAT'S AMAZING! I DIDN'T THINK YOU COULD DO IT, BUT I WAS WRONG! ♡
EH...?
AH...
YES.
BUT IT WAS JUST STAYING OVER...
HEY!! HARIMA!!!
WHAT DO YOU WANT, GLASSES?
YOU BAASSTTA-ARRDD!!!
WHOOM
WHAT'S THIS? SUDDENLY ATTACKING FOR NO REASON!

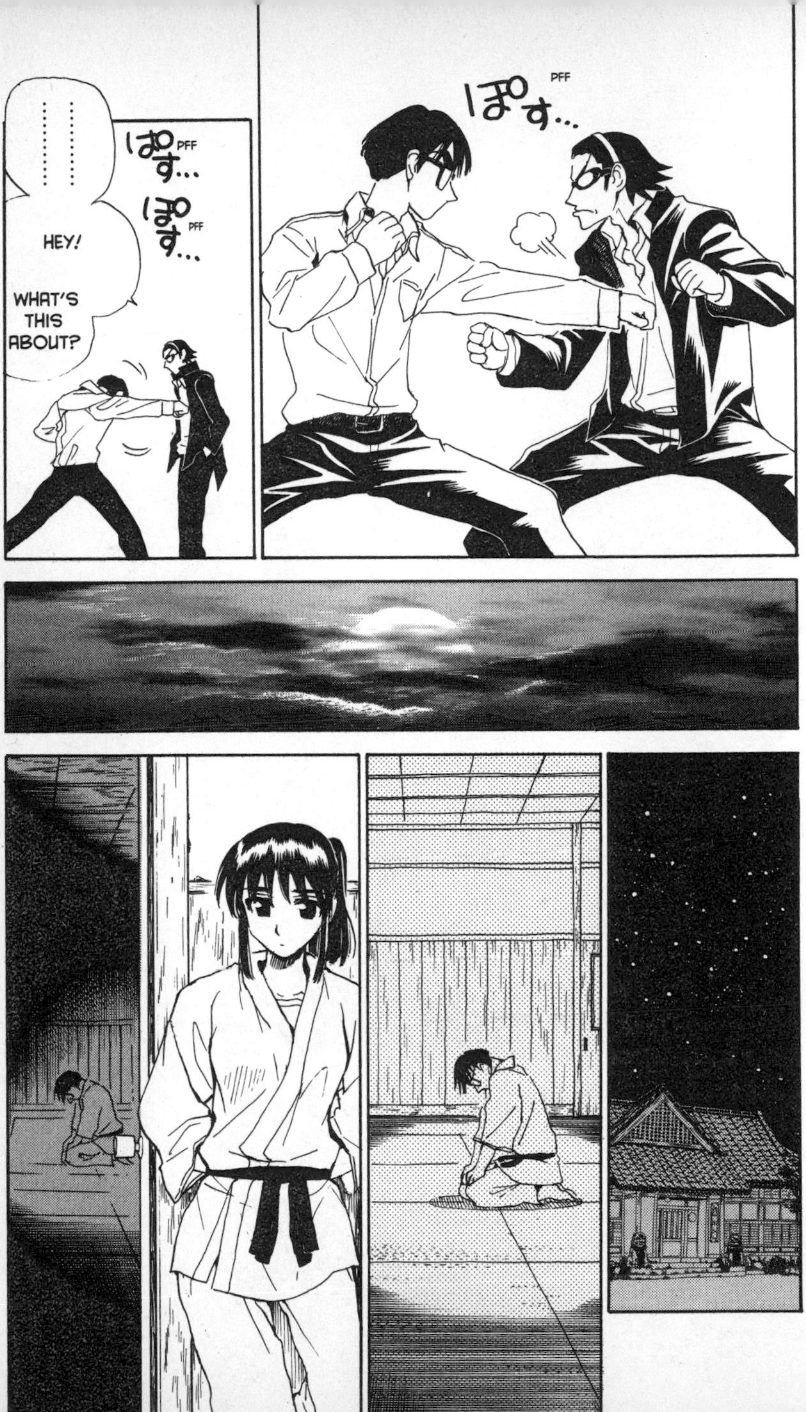
ぽす… PFF
ぽす… PFF
ぽす… PFF
HEY!
WHAT'S THIS ABOUT?
……
……

Suô Mikoto: Hanai's Childhood Friend.

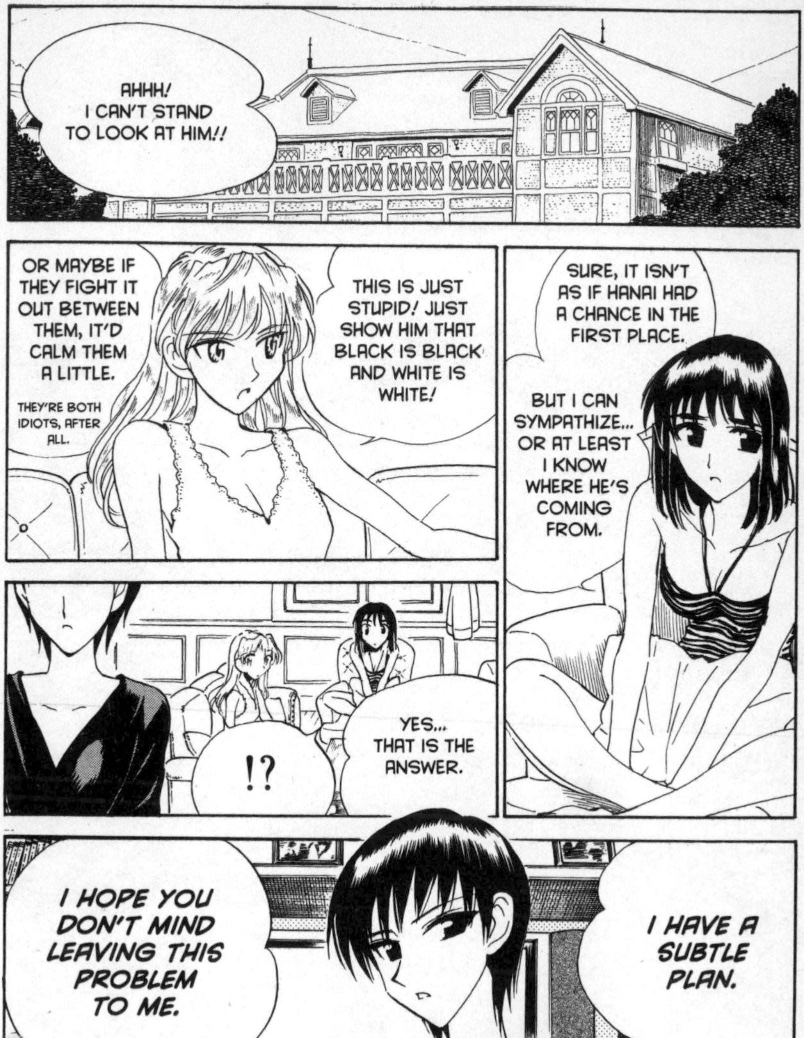
AHHH! I CAN'T STAND TO LOOK AT HIM!!
SURE, IT ISN'T AS IF HANAI HAD A CHANCE IN THE FIRST PLACE.
BUT I CAN SYMPATHIZE... OR AT LEAST I KNOW WHERE HE'S COMING FROM.
THIS IS JUST STUPID! JUST SHOW HIM THAT BLACK IS BLACK AND WHITE IS WHITE!
OR MAYBE IF THEY FIGHT IT OUT BETWEEN THEM, IT'D CALM THEM A LITTLE.
THEY'RE BOTH IDIOTS, AFTER ALL.
YES... THAT IS THE ANSWER.
!?
I HAVE A SUBTLE PLAN.
I HOPE YOU DON'T MIND LEAVING THIS PROBLEM TO ME.

Takano Akira: Joins the Fray.

 # 100 . . . . . Fin

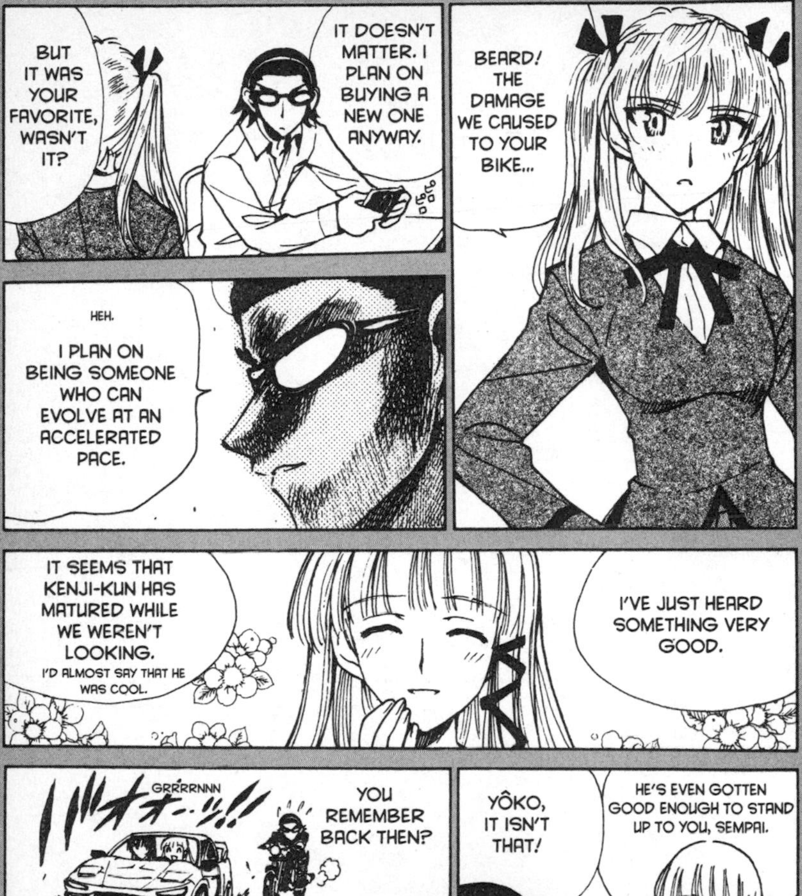
BEARD! THE DAMAGE WE CAUSED TO YOUR BIKE...
IT DOESN'T MATTER. I PLAN ON BUYING A NEW ONE ANYWAY.
BUT IT WAS YOUR FAVORITE, WASN'T IT?
HEH.
I PLAN ON BEING SOMEONE WHO CAN EVOLVE AT AN ACCELERATED PACE.
I'VE JUST HEARD SOMETHING VERY GOOD.
IT SEEMS THAT KENJI-KUN HAS MATURED WHILE WE WEREN'T LOOKING.
I'D ALMOST SAY THAT HE WAS COOL.
HE'S EVEN GOTTEN GOOD ENOUGH TO STAND UP TO YOU, SEMPAI.
YÔKO, IT ISN'T THAT!
YOU REMEMBER BACK THEN?
GRRRRNNN
YAAAY! WE WIN!!
REMEMBER WHEN WE HAD THAT STUPID, CHILDISH RACE?
HE WAS SO FRUSTRATED THAT HE LOST.

Original Bonus Manga Number 1

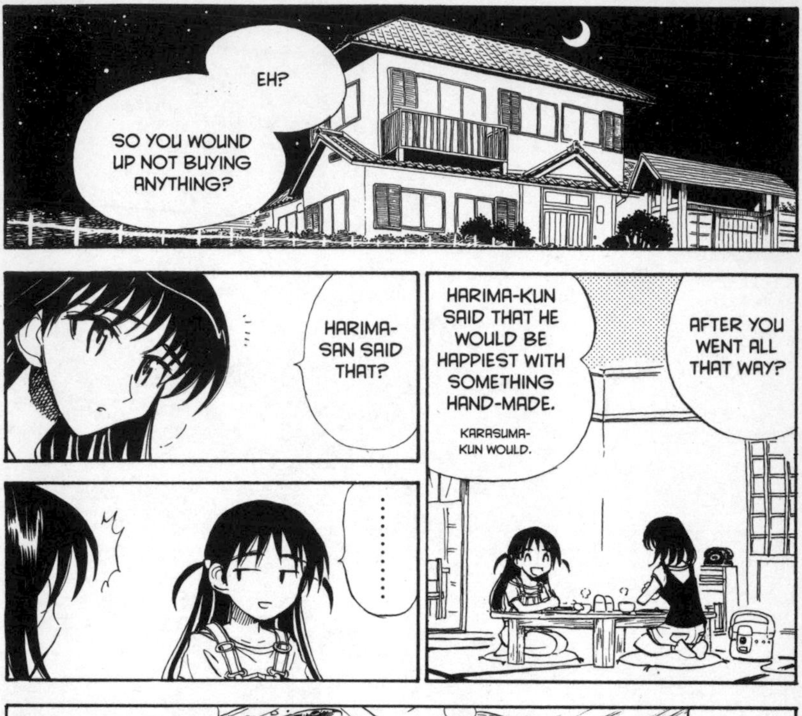
EH?
SO YOU WOUND UP NOT BUYING ANYTHING?
AFTER YOU WENT ALL THAT WAY?
HARIMA-KUN SAID THAT HE WOULD BE HAPPIEST WITH SOMETHING HAND-MADE.
KARASUMA-KUN WOULD.
HARIMA-SAN SAID THAT?
......
DON'T LET IT BOTHER YOU!!
I WOULD NEVER LAY A FINGER ON YOUR HARIMA-KUN!!
EH...! NO!
UM...
THAT ISN'T WHAT I MEANT...!
COME ON! I ONLY BORROWED HIM FOR AN AFTERNOON! I NEVER THOUGHT YOU'D BE THAT POSSESSIVE, YAKUMO!
DON'T BE SO JEALOUS, YOU!
NO. YOU'VE GOT IT WRONG...
I'VE GOT WHAT WRONG?
Y—
YOU'VE GOT...

#101 TOO HOT TO HANDLE

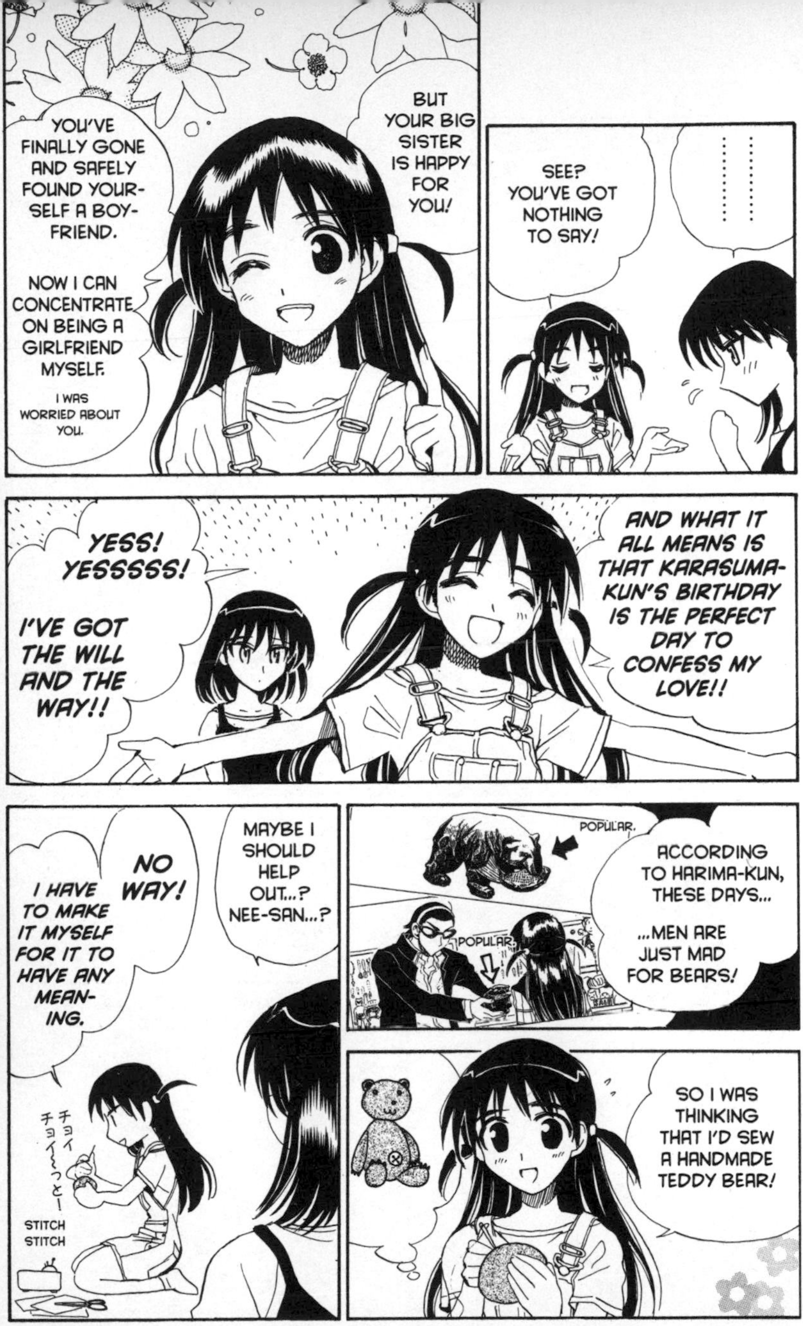
......
SEE? YOU'VE GOT NOTHING TO SAY!
BUT YOUR BIG SISTER IS HAPPY FOR YOU!
YOU'VE FINALLY GONE AND SAFELY FOUND YOURSELF A BOY-FRIEND.
NOW I CAN CONCENTRATE ON BEING A GIRLFRIEND MYSELF.
I WAS WORRIED ABOUT YOU.
AND WHAT IT ALL MEANS IS THAT KARASUMA-KUN'S BIRTHDAY IS THE PERFECT DAY TO CONFESS MY LOVE!!
YESS! YESSSSS!
I'VE GOT THE WILL AND THE WAY!!
POPULAR.
POPULAR.
ACCORDING TO HARIMA-KUN, THESE DAYS...
...MEN ARE JUST MAD FOR BEARS!
SO I WAS THINKING THAT I'D SEW A HANDMADE TEDDY BEAR!
MAYBE I SHOULD HELP OUT...? NEE-SAN...?
NO WAY!
I HAVE TO MAKE IT MYSELF FOR IT TO HAVE ANY MEAN-ING.
チョイチョイ～っと－
STITCH STITCH

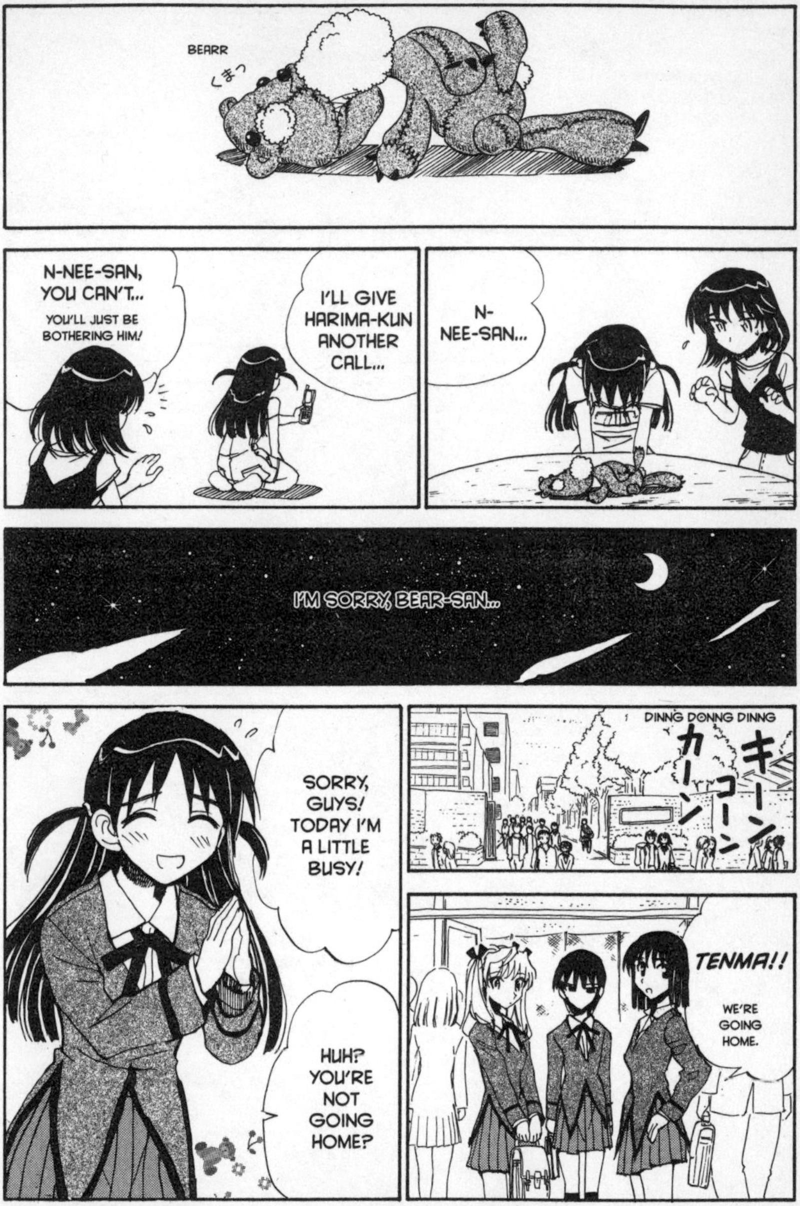
BEARR
くまっ
N-NEE-SAN...
I'LL GIVE HARIMA-KUN ANOTHER CALL...
N-NEE-SAN, YOU CAN'T...
YOU'LL JUST BE BOTHERING HIM!
I'M SORRY, BEAR-SAN...
DINNG DONNG DINNG
キーンコーンカーン
TENMA!!
WE'RE GOING HOME.
SORRY, GUYS! TODAY I'M A LITTLE BUSY!
HUH? YOU'RE NOT GOING HOME?

Splatter.

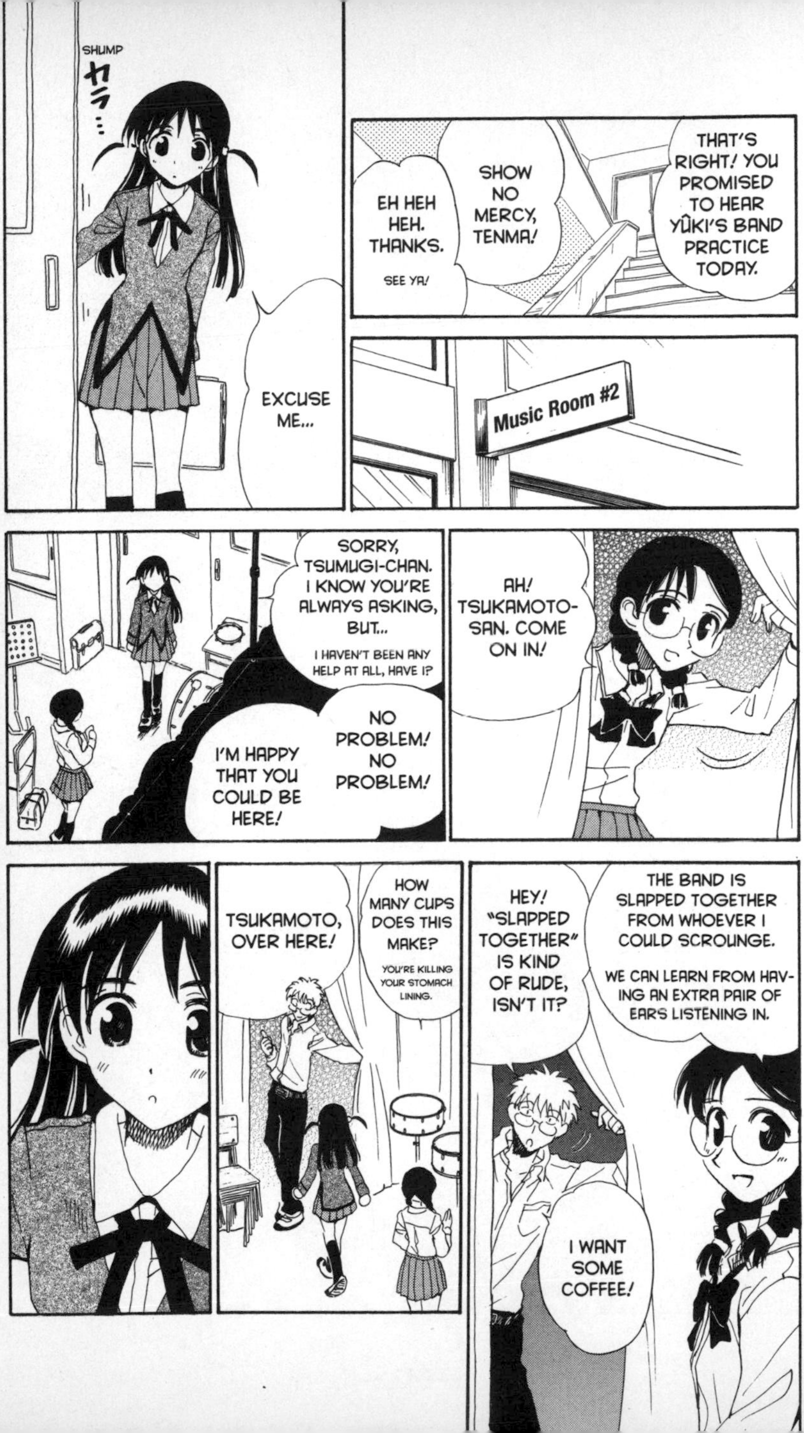
THAT'S RIGHT! YOU PROMISED TO HEAR YÛKI'S BAND PRACTICE TODAY.
SHOW NO MERCY, TENMA!
EH HEH HEH. THANKS.
SEE YA!
Music Room #2
SHUMP
カラ…
EXCUSE ME...
AH! TSUKAMOTO-SAN. COME ON IN!
SORRY, TSUMUGI-CHAN. I KNOW YOU'RE ALWAYS ASKING, BUT...
I HAVEN'T BEEN ANY HELP AT ALL, HAVE I?
NO PROBLEM! NO PROBLEM!
I'M HAPPY THAT YOU COULD BE HERE!
THE BAND IS SLAPPED TOGETHER FROM WHOEVER I COULD SCROUNGE.
WE CAN LEARN FROM HAVING AN EXTRA PAIR OF EARS LISTENING IN.
HEY! "SLAPPED TOGETHER" IS KIND OF RUDE, ISN'T IT?
I WANT SOME COFFEE!
HOW MANY CUPS DOES THIS MAKE?
YOU'RE KILLING YOUR STOMACH LINING.
TSUKAMOTO, OVER HERE!

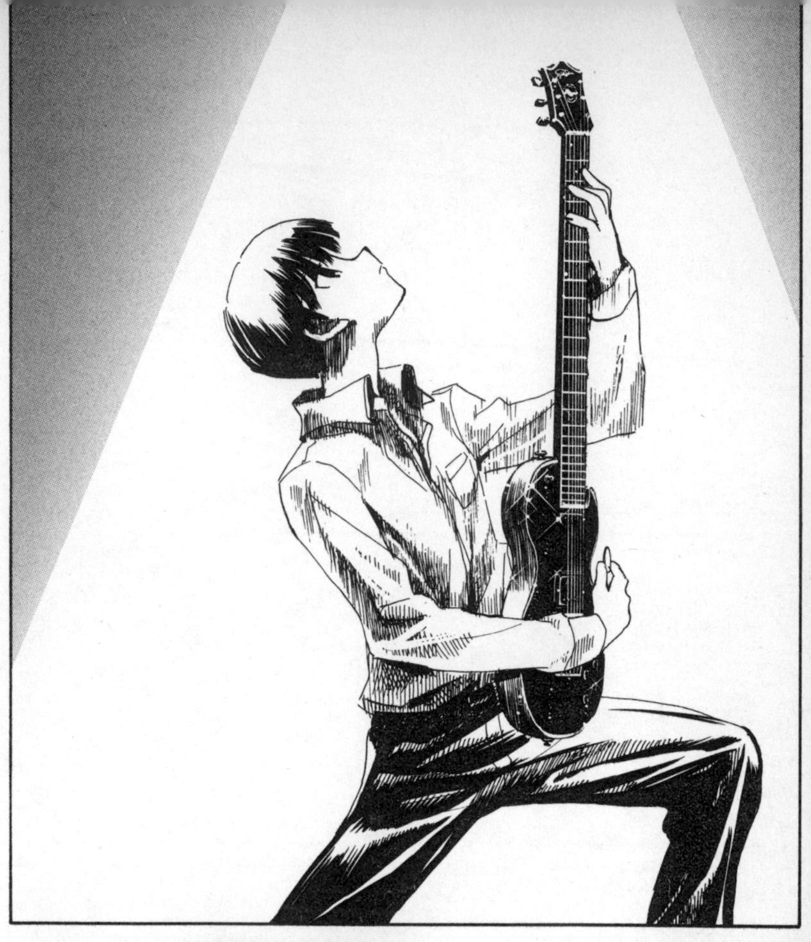

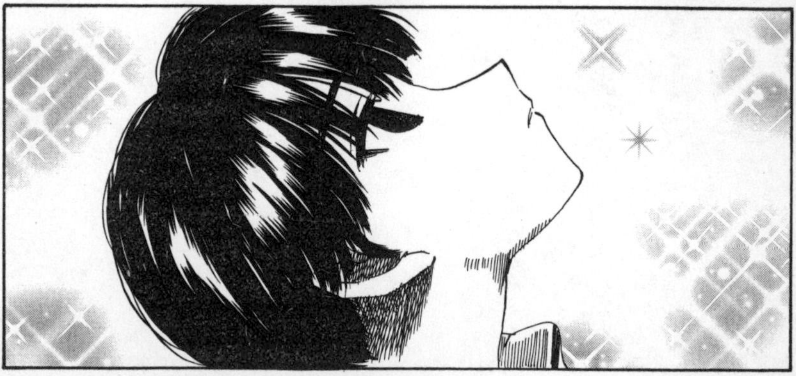

Karasuma Ôji: Tenma's Classmate and Love. Just a Basic Fact.

DON'T YOU HAVE A POSE, TSUMUGI-CHAN?

EH?!

RIGHT! NOW MOVE YOUR LEG A LITTLE THIS WAY...

HMM. I THINK YOU'VE ALMOST GOT IT!

JUST MOVE THIS RIGHT HERE.

I THINK THAT WILL MAKE A SLIGHTLY BETTER PICTURE.

IT WAS AN IDEA OFF THE TOP OF FUYUKI-KUN'S HEAD.

NOTHING MORE THAN THAT.

I GOT ROPED INTO IT.

IT'S A REALLY INTERESTING IDEA FOR A CULTURALLY ORIENTED CLUB TO FORM A BAND.

AH! KARERIN ISN'T IN THE CLUB, IS SHE?

H—

HOW ABOUT THIS...

MAYBE?

MOVEMENTS ON THE KEYBOARD AREN'T REALLY IMPRESSIVE...

IT'S TRUE! YOU'RE ALL DOING GREAT!

STILL, WITH SOME HONEST REHEARSAL, WE WON'T MAKE FOOLS OF OURSELVES.

WOW!! THAT'S GREAT! THAT'S THE ONE!

IT'S REALLY COOL!

YEAH... WE HAD TO FORCE HER INTO IT A LITTLE.

A FEW DIFFERENT WAYS.

BUT SHE SAID SHE'D DO IT?

KARERIN DID?

I WENT TO KARAOKE WITH HER, AND I WAS SHOCKED!

ICHIJÔ CAN REALLY SING!

KARASUMA AND ICHIJÔ REALLY SURPRISED ME!

THEY'RE AMAZING!

Fuyuki Takeichi: Ero-Photographer.

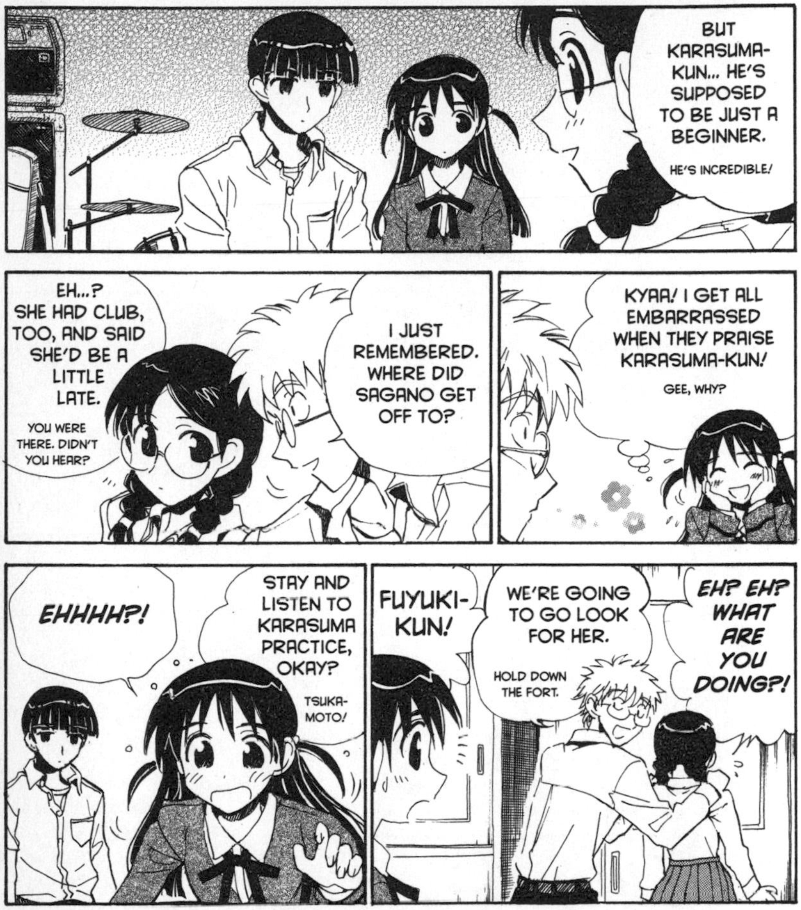
BUT KARASUMA-KUN... HE'S SUPPOSED TO BE JUST A BEGINNER.
HE'S INCREDIBLE!
KYAA! I GET ALL EMBARRASSED WHEN THEY PRAISE KARASUMA-KUN!
GEE, WHY?
I JUST REMEMBERED. WHERE DID SAGANO GET OFF TO?
EH...? SHE HAD CLUB, TOO, AND SAID SHE'D BE A LITTLE LATE.
YOU WERE THERE. DIDN'T YOU HEAR?
EH? EH? WHAT ARE YOU DOING?!
WE'RE GOING TO GO LOOK FOR HER.
HOLD DOWN THE FORT.
FUYUKI-KUN!
STAY AND LISTEN TO KARASUMA PRACTICE, OKAY?
TSUKA-MOTO!
EHHHH?!
YOU REALLY ACT LIKE YOU'RE STILL IN JUNIOR HIGH, FUYUKI-KUN!
I KNOW WHERE YOU'RE COMING FROM, BUT...
DON'T TALK LIKE THAT!
WE HAVE TO GET THEM TALKING, EVEN IF THEY'RE FORCED INTO IT.
THOSE TWO.

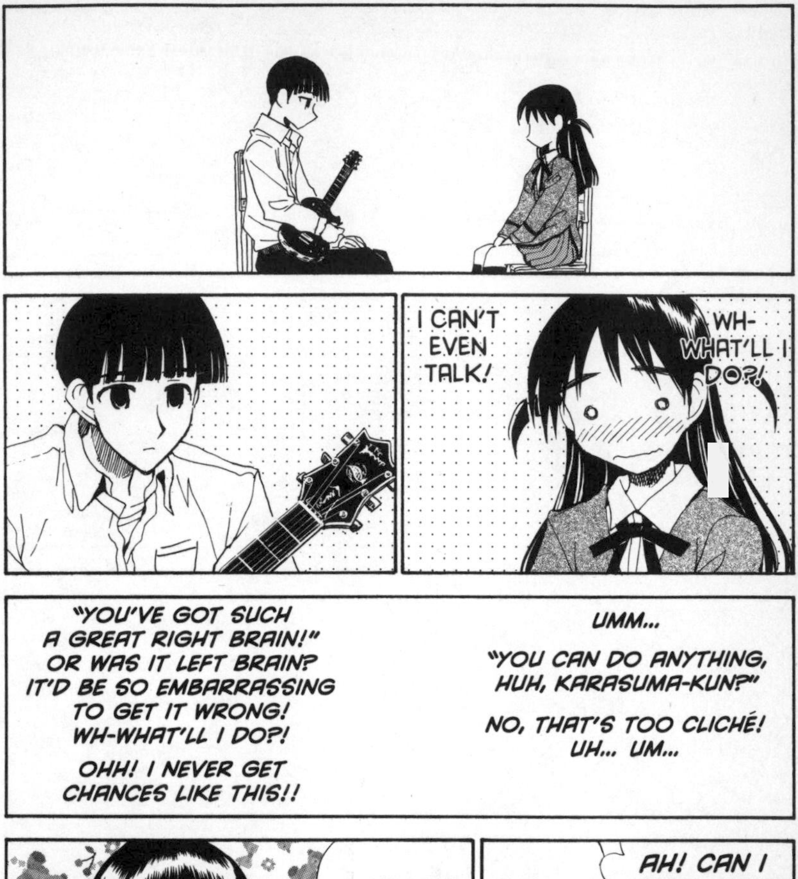
WH-WHAT'LL I DO?!
I CAN'T EVEN TALK!
UMM...
"YOU CAN DO ANYTHING, HUH, KARASUMA-KUN?"
NO, THAT'S TOO CLICHÉ! UH... UM...
"YOU'VE GOT SUCH A GREAT RIGHT BRAIN!" OR WAS IT LEFT BRAIN? IT'D BE SO EMBARRASSING TO GET IT WRONG! WH-WHAT'LL I DO?!
OHH! I NEVER GET CHANCES LIKE THIS!!
AH! CAN I HOLD YOUR GUITAR?
YEAH.
I-IS THIS HOW YOU PLAY IT?!

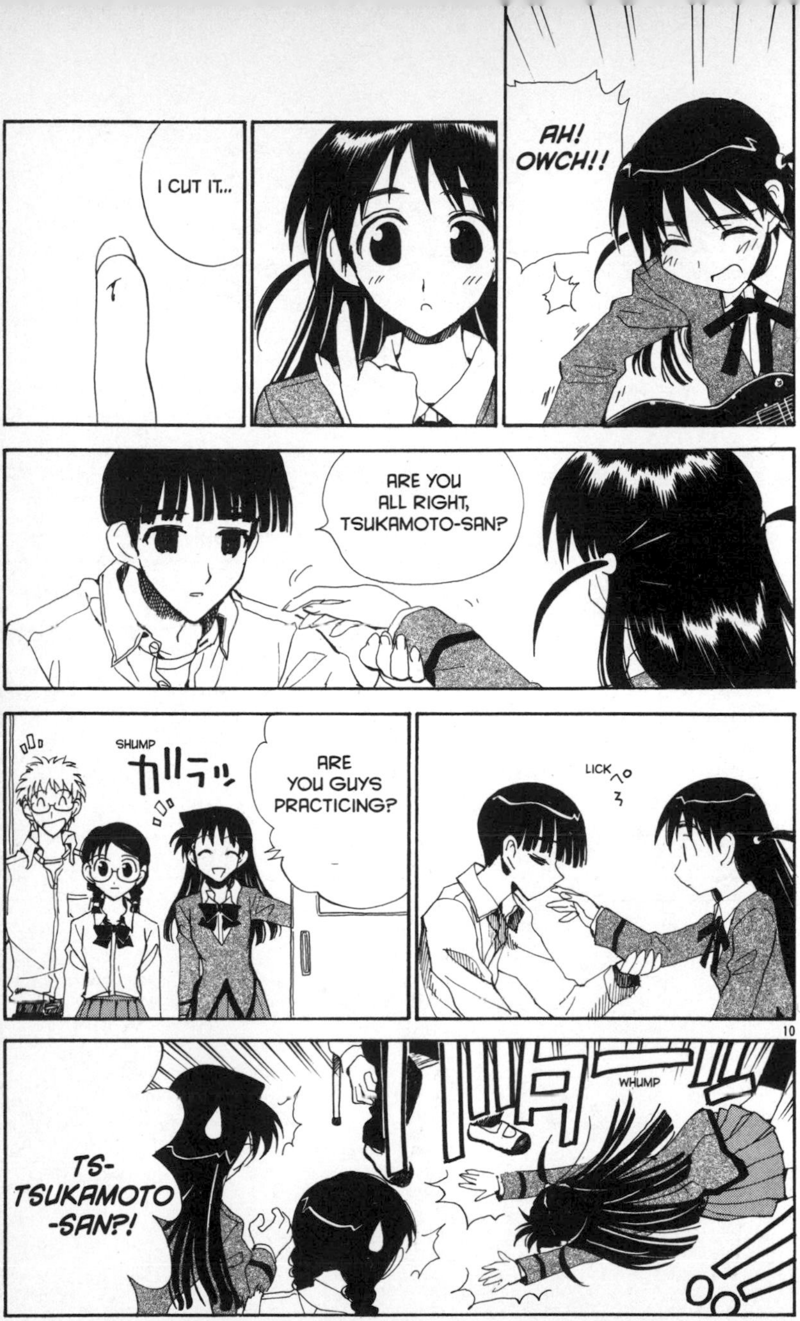
AH! OWCH!!
I CUT IT...
ARE YOU ALL RIGHT, TSUKAMOTO-SAN?
LICK
ARE YOU GUYS PRACTICING?
SHUMP
ガラッ
10
WHUMP
TS-TSUKAMOTO -SAN?!

And She Got Another Nosebleed.

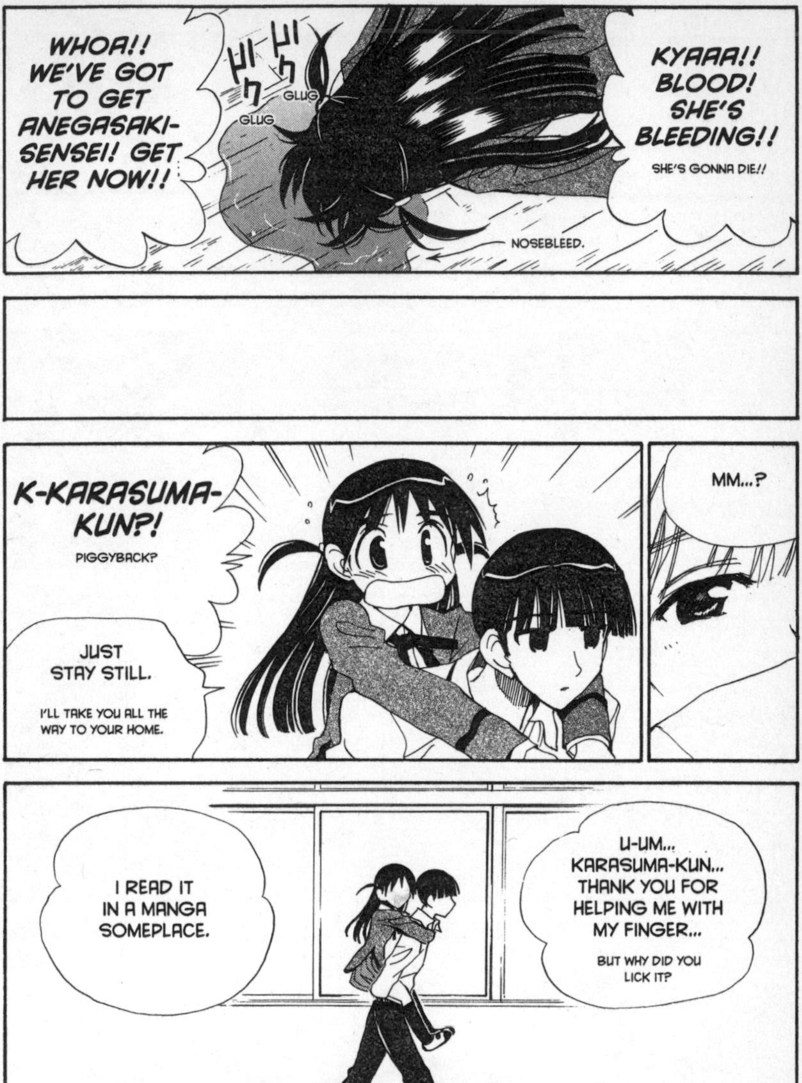

KYAAA!! BLOOD! SHE'S BLEEDING!!
SHE'S GONNA DIE!!
GLUG
GLUG
NOSEBLEED.
WHOA!! WE'VE GOT TO GET ANEGASAKI-SENSEI! GET HER NOW!!
MM...?
K-KARASUMA-KUN?!
PIGGYBACK?
JUST STAY STILL.
I'LL TAKE YOU ALL THE WAY TO YOUR HOME.
U-UM... KARASUMA-KUN... THANK YOU FOR HELPING ME WITH MY FINGER...
BUT WHY DID YOU LICK IT?
I READ IT IN A MANGA SOMEPLACE.

101 · · · · · · · · ·Fin

#102 JOHNNY GOT HIS GUN

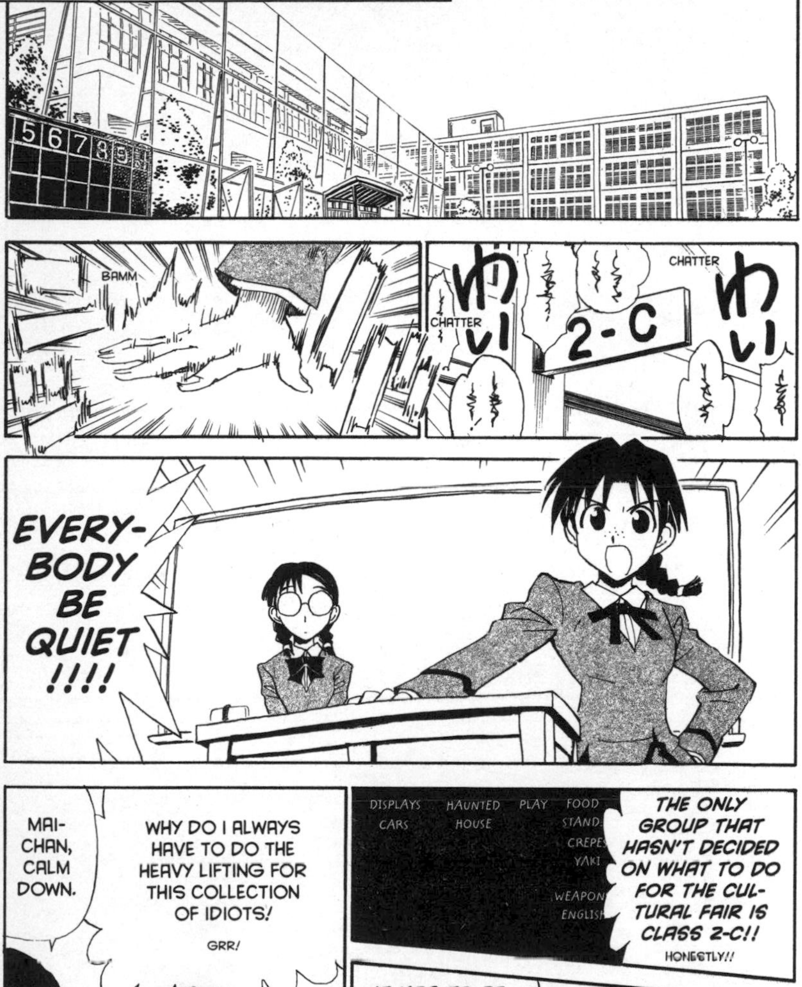

わい
CHATTER
2-C
わい
CHATTER
BAMM
EVERY-BODY BE QUIET!!!!
DISPLAYS
CARS
HAUNTED HOUSE
PLAY
FOOD STANDS
CREPES
YAKI
WEAPON
ENGLISH
THE ONLY GROUP THAT HASN'T DECIDED ON WHAT TO DO FOR THE CULTURAL FAIR IS CLASS 2-C!!
HONESTLY!!
IT HAS TO BE DECIDED BY TODAY, AND LOOK AT YOU GUYS!
PLAYING CARDS, HANAFUDA, MANGA, GAMES! THIS IS SCHOOL, PEOPLE!!
WHY DO I ALWAYS HAVE TO DO THE HEAVY LIFTING FOR THIS COLLECTION OF IDIOTS!
GRR!
MAI-CHAN, CALM DOWN.

Imadori Kyôsuke: Recently in Charge of Short Scenarios.

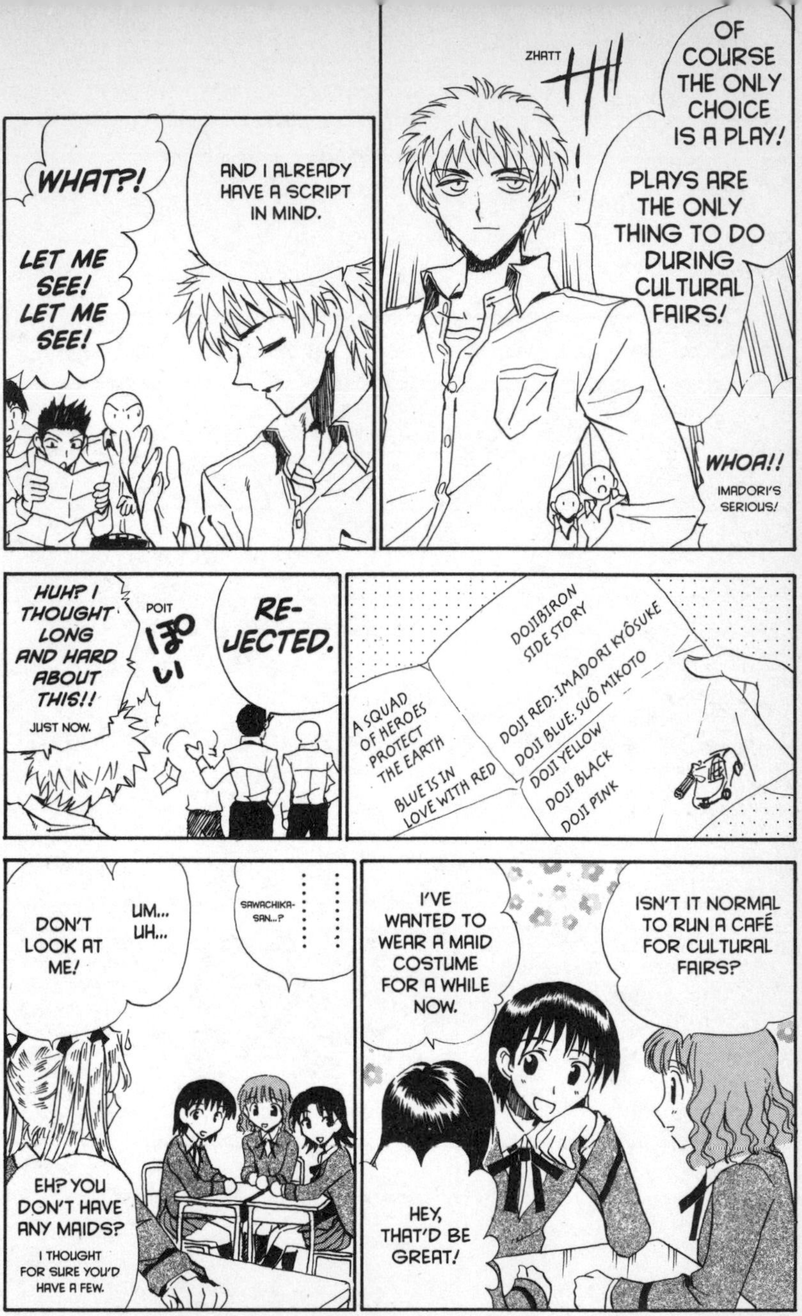
OF COURSE THE ONLY CHOICE IS A PLAY!
ZHATT
PLAYS ARE THE ONLY THING TO DO DURING CULTURAL FAIRS!
WHOA!!
IMADORI'S SERIOUS!
AND I ALREADY HAVE A SCRIPT IN MIND.
WHAT?!
LET ME SEE! LET ME SEE!
DOJIBIRON SIDE STORY
DOJI RED: IMADORI KYÔSUKE
DOJI BLUE: SUÔ MIKOTO
DOJI YELLOW
DOJI BLACK
DOJI PINK
A SQUAD OF HEROES PROTECT THE EARTH
BLUE IS IN LOVE WITH RED
RE-JECTED.
POIT
ぽい
HUH? I THOUGHT LONG AND HARD ABOUT THIS!!
JUST NOW.
ISN'T IT NORMAL TO RUN A CAFÉ FOR CULTURAL FAIRS?
I'VE WANTED TO WEAR A MAID COSTUME FOR A WHILE NOW.
HEY, THAT'D BE GREAT!
SAWACHIKA-SAN...?
UM... UH...
DON'T LOOK AT ME!
EH? YOU DON'T HAVE ANY MAIDS?
I THOUGHT FOR SURE YOU'D HAVE A FEW.

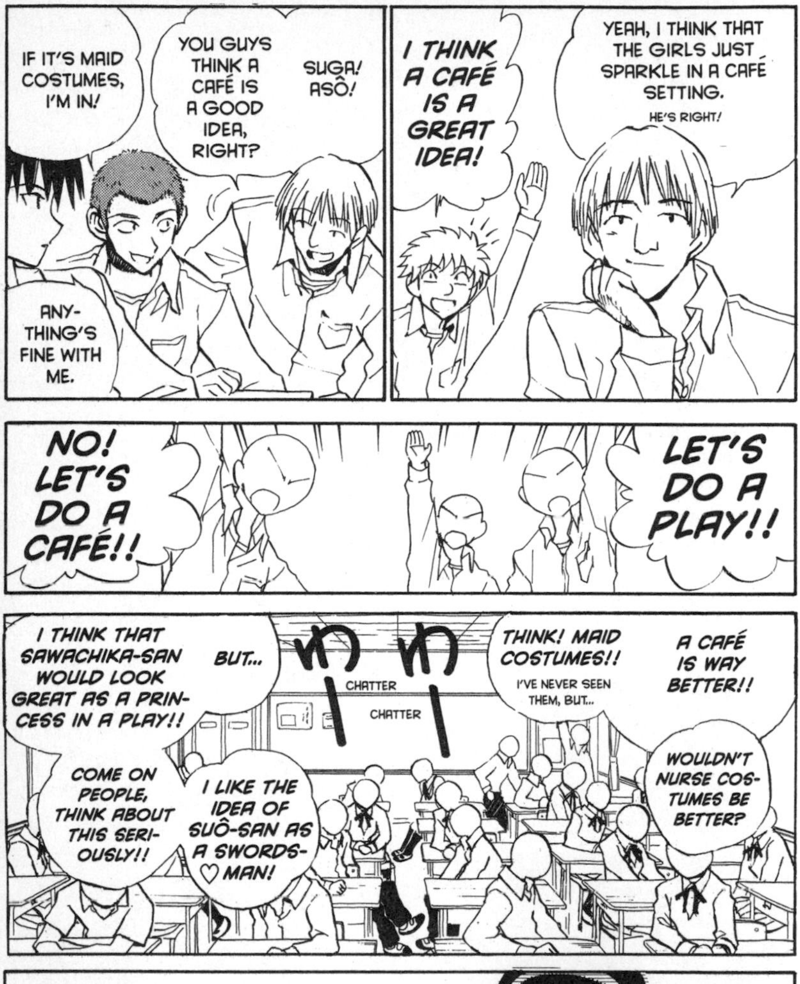
YEAH, I THINK THAT THE GIRLS JUST SPARKLE IN A CAFÉ SETTING.
HE'S RIGHT!
I THINK A CAFÉ IS A GREAT IDEA!
SUGA! ASÔ!
YOU GUYS THINK A CAFÉ IS A GOOD IDEA, RIGHT?
IF IT'S MAID COSTUMES, I'M IN!
ANY-THING'S FINE WITH ME.
LET'S DO A PLAY!!
NO! LET'S DO A CAFÉ!!
A CAFÉ IS WAY BETTER!!
THINK! MAID COSTUMES!!
I'VE NEVER SEEN THEM, BUT...
WOULDN'T NURSE COS-TUMES BE BETTER?
わー
CHATTER
わー
CHATTER
BUT...
I THINK THAT SAWACHIKA-SAN WOULD LOOK GREAT AS A PRIN-CESS IN A PLAY!!
I LIKE THE IDEA OF SUÔ-SAN AS A SWORDS-MAN! ♡
COME ON PEOPLE, THINK ABOUT THIS SERI-OUSLY!!
TSK! THEY MAKE SO MUCH NOISE!
WHO CARES ABOUT THE DUMB CULTURAL FAIR? I HAVE TO STUDY!
EVEN IF IT IS MAKE-UPS.

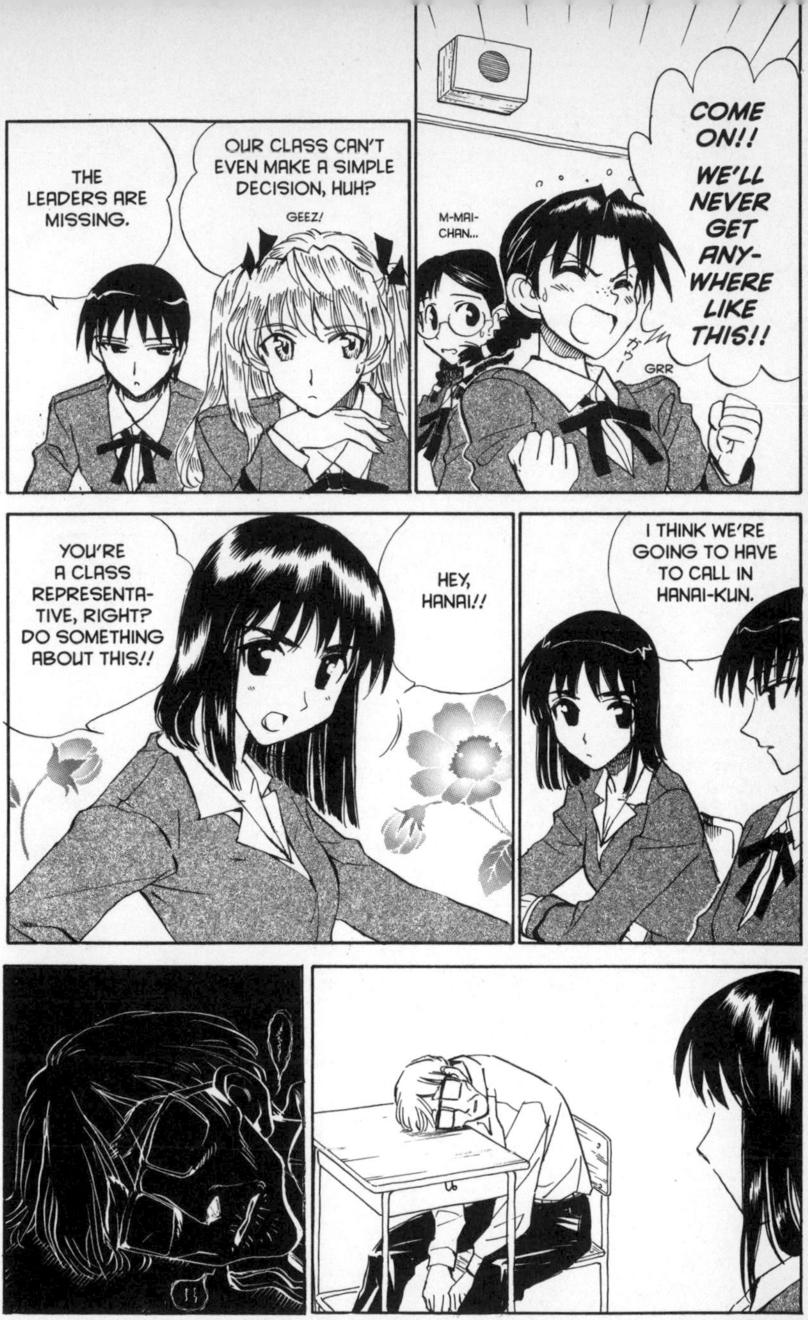
COME ON!! WE'LL NEVER GET ANYWHERE LIKE THIS!!
M-MAI-CHAN...
GRR
OUR CLASS CAN'T EVEN MAKE A SIMPLE DECISION, HUH?
GEEZ!
THE LEADERS ARE MISSING.
I THINK WE'RE GOING TO HAVE TO CALL IN HANAI-KUN.
HEY, HANAI!!
YOU'RE A CLASS REPRESENTATIVE, RIGHT? DO SOMETHING ABOUT THIS!!

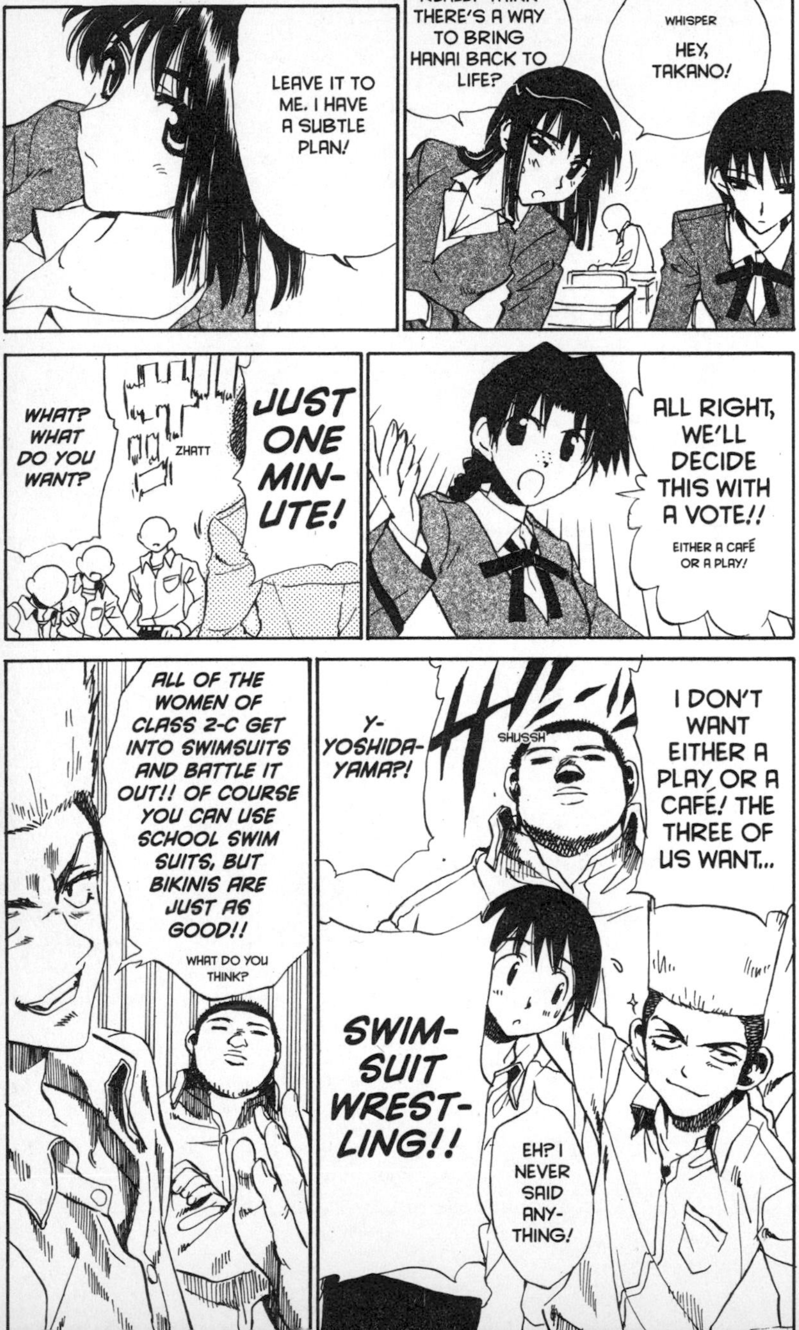
WHISPER
HEY, TAKANO!
DO YOU REALLY THINK THERE'S A WAY TO BRING HANAI BACK TO LIFE?
LEAVE IT TO ME. I HAVE A SUBTLE PLAN!
ALL RIGHT, WE'LL DECIDE THIS WITH A VOTE!!
EITHER A CAFÉ OR A PLAY!
JUST ONE MIN-UTE!
ZHATT
WHAT? WHAT DO YOU WANT?
I DON'T WANT EITHER A PLAY OR A CAFÉ! THE THREE OF US WANT...
SHUSSH
Y-YOSHIDA-YAMA?!
SWIM-SUIT WREST-LING!!
EH? I NEVER SAID ANY-THING!
ALL OF THE WOMEN OF CLASS 2-C GET INTO SWIMSUITS AND BATTLE IT OUT!! OF COURSE YOU CAN USE SCHOOL SWIM SUITS, BUT BIKINIS ARE JUST AS GOOD!!
WHAT DO YOU THINK?

Yoshidayama Jirô: A Self-Styled Juvenile Delinquent.

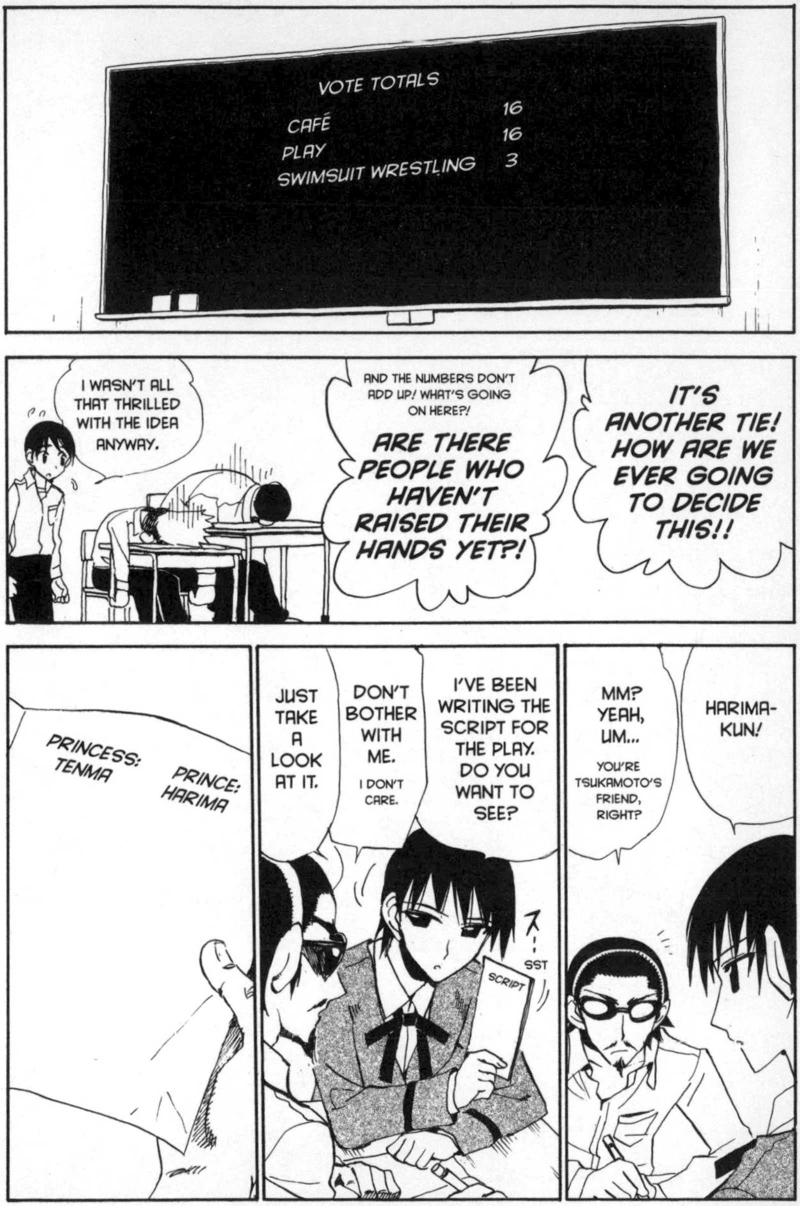
VOTE TOTALS
CAFÉ 16
PLAY 16
SWIMSUIT WRESTLING 3
IT'S ANOTHER TIE! HOW ARE WE EVER GOING TO DECIDE THIS!!
AND THE NUMBERS DON'T ADD UP! WHAT'S GOING ON HERE?!
ARE THERE PEOPLE WHO HAVEN'T RAISED THEIR HANDS YET?!
I WASN'T ALL THAT THRILLED WITH THE IDEA ANYWAY.
HARIMA-KUN!
MM? YEAH, UM...
YOU'RE TSUKAMOTO'S FRIEND, RIGHT?
I'VE BEEN WRITING THE SCRIPT FOR THE PLAY. DO YOU WANT TO SEE?
DON'T BOTHER WITH ME.
I DON'T CARE.
JUST TAKE A LOOK AT IT.
SST
SCRIPT
PRINCESS: TENMA
PRINCE: HARIMA

Ero Committee: No Force Behind It.

BAMM

HARIMA KENJI CASTS THREE VOTES FOR THE PLAY!!!

SOME OF THIS, SOME OF THAT.

TAKANO, WHAT DID YOU JUST SAY TO HIM?

THAT DECIDES IT!!

I DON'T KNOW WHY HE GETS THREE VOTES, BUT...

WOW! THREE VOTES AT ONCE!!

CHATTER CHATTER

I'M NOT FINISHED YET.

WHAT GOOD WILL IT DO TO STIR UP HARIMA?

IT'S THE PLAY!!

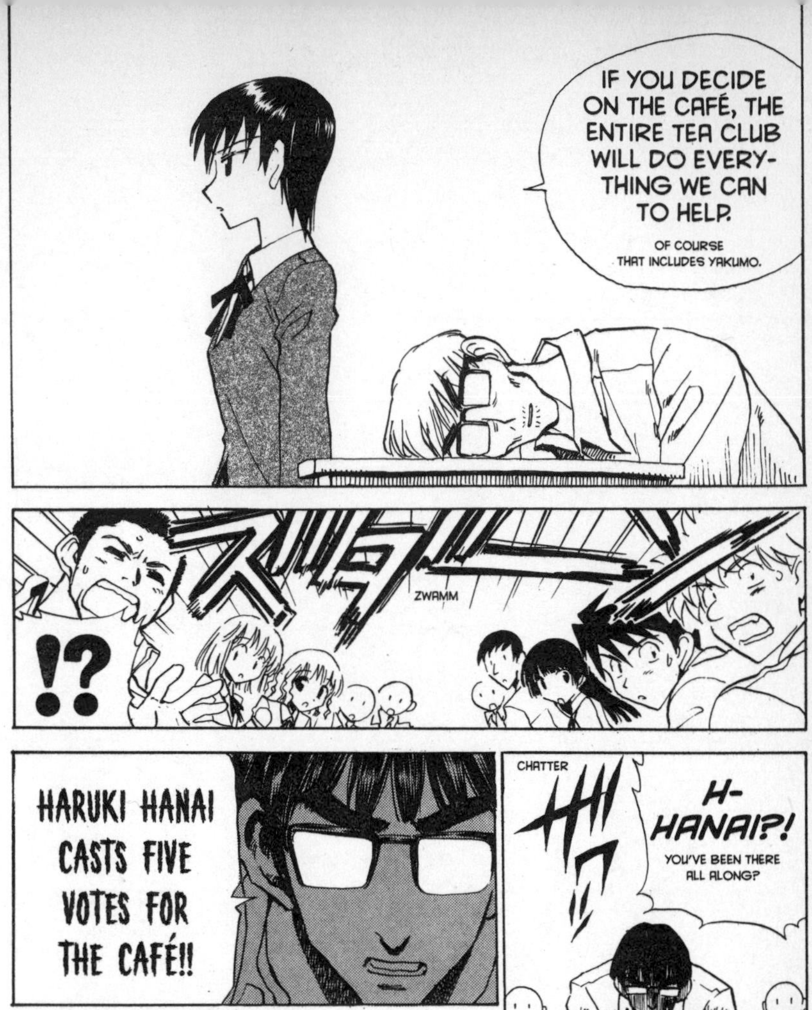
IF YOU DECIDE ON THE CAFÉ, THE ENTIRE TEA CLUB WILL DO EVERY-THING WE CAN TO HELP.
OF COURSE THAT INCLUDES YAKUMO.
ZWAMM
!?
CHATTER
H-HANAI?!
YOU'VE BEEN THERE ALL ALONG?
HARUKI HANAI CASTS FIVE VOTES FOR THE CAFÉ!!
F-FIVE VOTES?!
THERE IT IS!!
A COME-FROM-BEHIND VICTORY!!
わああっ!!
WHOORAA
WHY DOES HE GET TO CAST 5 VOTES?

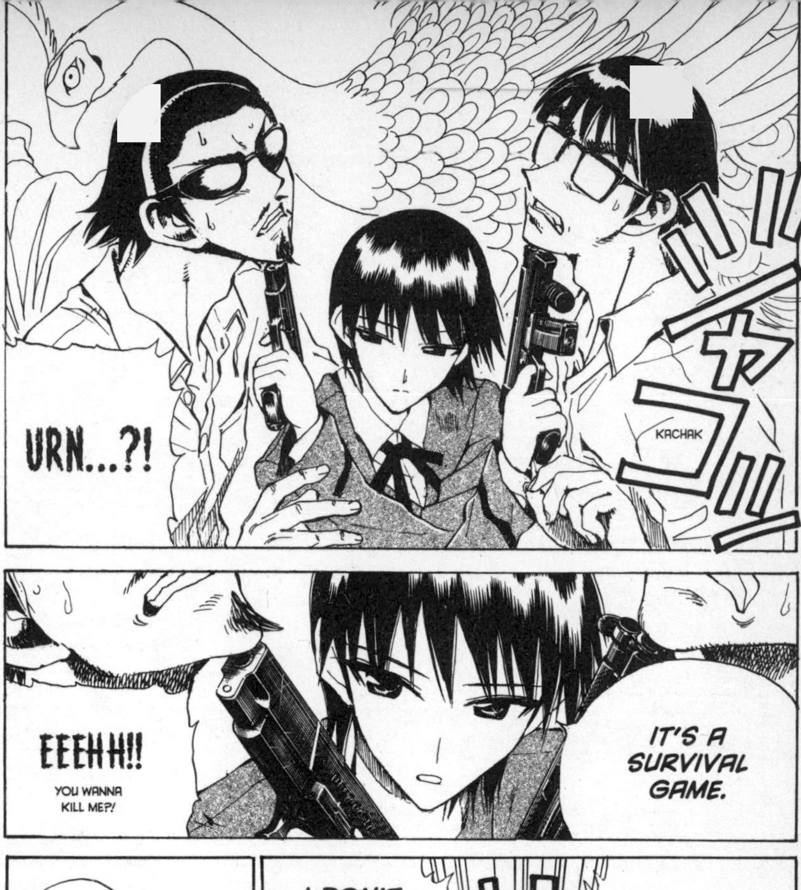
URN...?!
KACHAK
IT'S A SURVIVAL GAME.
EEEHH!!
YOU WANNA KILL ME?!
DID YOU SAY A SURVIVAL GAME?!
CHATTER
I DON'T KNOW WHAT IT IS, BUT I THINK IT'LL DECIDE THINGS!!
I GET THE FEELING THIS ARGUMENT IS HEADED IN THE WRONG DIRECTION.
WHAAAH!
MAI-CHAN, IT DOES NO GOOD TO RESIGN NOW...
I DON'T CARE ANYMORE!

Ah . . . Tenma.

102 . . . . .Fin

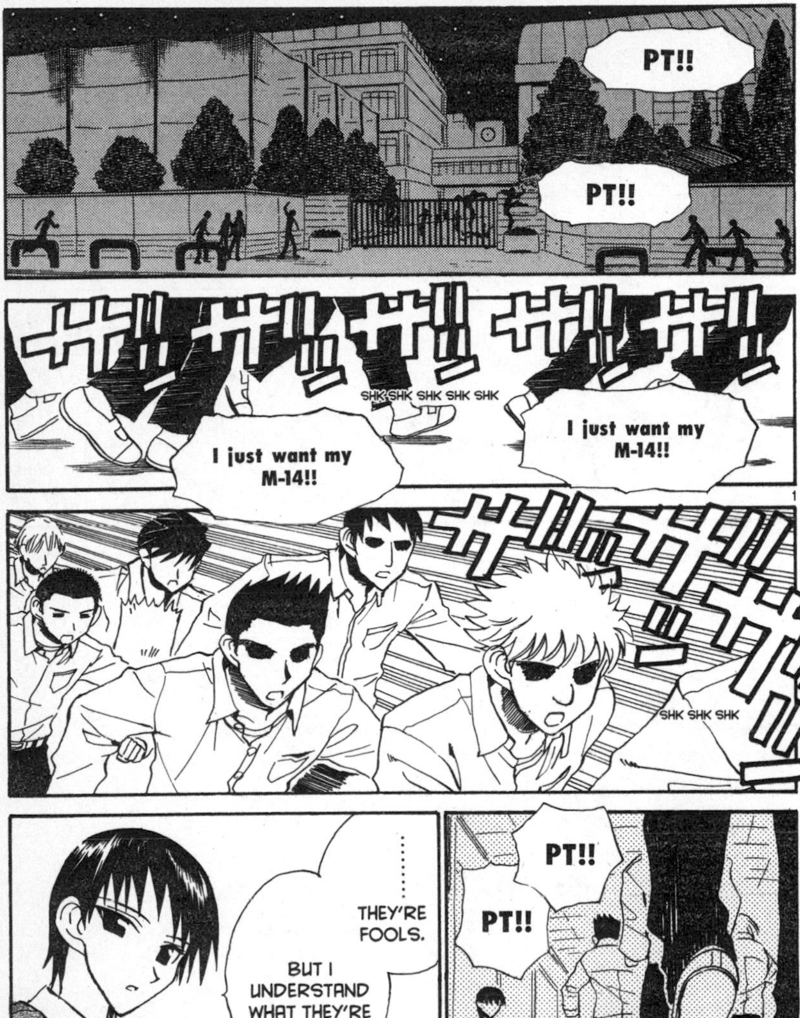
PT!!
PT!!
SHK SHK SHK SHK SHK
I just want my M-14!!
I just want my M-14!!
SHK SHK SHK
PT!!
PT!!
......
THEY'RE FOOLS.
BUT I UNDERSTAND WHAT THEY'RE FEELING.
KACHAK

#103 THE DOGS OF WAR

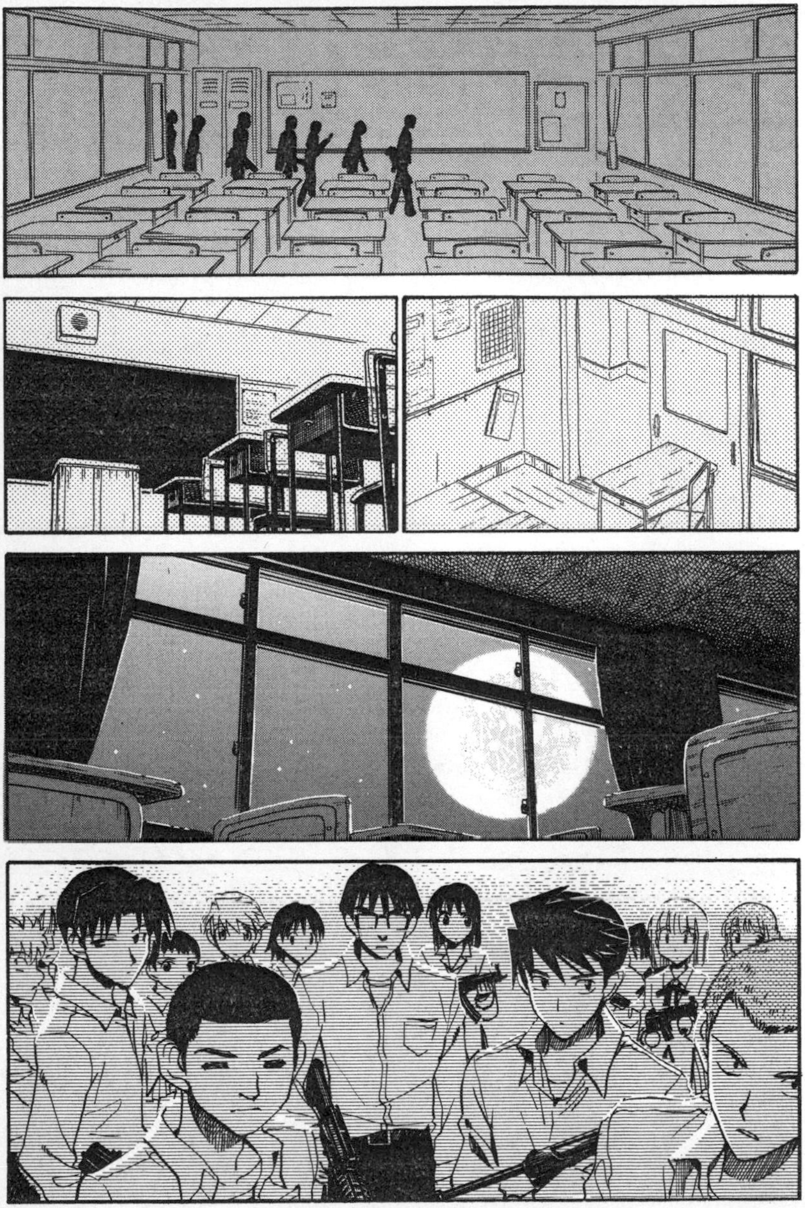

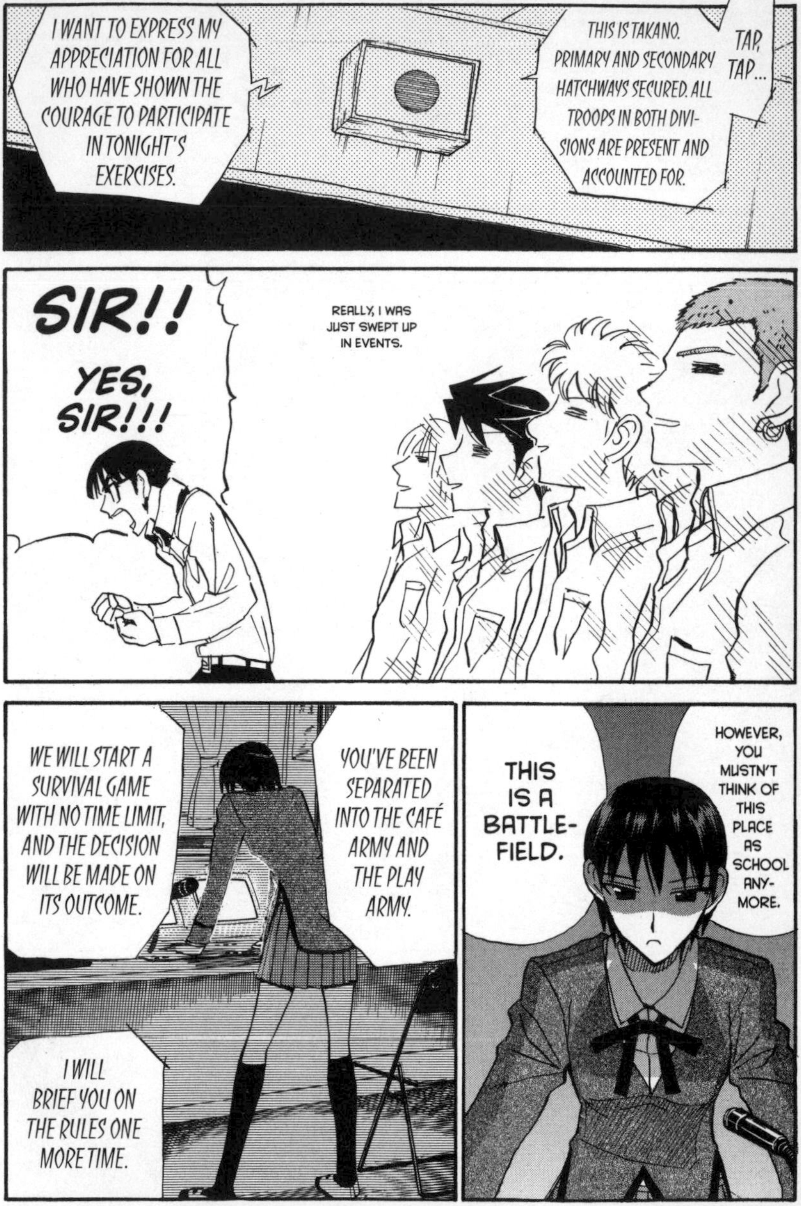
TAP, TAP...
THIS IS TAKANO. PRIMARY AND SECONDARY HATCHWAYS SECURED. ALL TROOPS IN BOTH DIVISIONS ARE PRESENT AND ACCOUNTED FOR.
I WANT TO EXPRESS MY APPRECIATION FOR ALL WHO HAVE SHOWN THE COURAGE TO PARTICIPATE IN TONIGHT'S EXERCISES.
REALLY, I WAS JUST SWEPT UP IN EVENTS.
SIR!!
YES, SIR!!!
HOWEVER, YOU MUSTN'T THINK OF THIS PLACE AS SCHOOL ANYMORE.
THIS IS A BATTLEFIELD.
YOU'VE BEEN SEPARATED INTO THE CAFÉ ARMY AND THE PLAY ARMY.
WE WILL START A SURVIVAL GAME WITH NO TIME LIMIT, AND THE DECISION WILL BE MADE ON ITS OUTCOME.
I WILL BRIEF YOU ON THE RULES ONE MORE TIME.

Hanai Haruki: Completely Revived.

School Rumble.

THE FLAGS FOR BOTH ARMIES ARE IN THEIR PRESENT BASE LOCATIONS.

EACH ARMY WILL TRY TO STEAL THE ENEMY ARMY'S FLAG. THE ARMY THAT IS SUCCESSFUL FIRST WILL CLAIM VICTORY.

THESE ARE THE SAME FLAGS YOU VIEWED YESTERDAY.

IN OTHER WORDS, THEY ARE ON OPPOSITE SIDES OF SCHOOL BUILDING A.

THE CAFÉ ARMY HAS TAKEN POSITION IN 3-F, WHILE THE PLAY ARMY IS ENTRENCHED IN 1-A.

3-F

4F
3F
2F
1F

1-A

WHILE THE BATTLE CONTINUES, ANY WHO ARE HIT BY THE ENEMY'S— OR FRIENDLY—BBS WILL BE CONSIDERED TO HAVE DIED IN BATTLE.

A HIT ON ONE'S EQUIPMENT OR ANYWHERE ON ONE'S BODY WILL BE CONSIDERED A KILL. THEY WILL DROP OUT OF THE GAME.

HOWEVER, RICOCHETING BBS DON'T COUNT.

STEALING THE FLAG IS THE OBJECT OF THIS GAME.

IN OTHER WORDS, TO TAKE THE ENEMY'S FLAG, ONE WILL HAVE TO INFILTRATE THE ENEMY'S BASE.

THERE ARE NO OFF-LIMITS AREAS. CREATE YOUR OWN BARRICADES IF THEY FIT YOUR PLANS.

HOWEVER, DO NOT DESTROY SCHOOL PROPERTY.

ONE MAY USE SEMI-AUTOMATIC OR FULLY AUTOMATIC FIRE. HOWEVER, ALTERED WEAPONS WILL NOT BE PERMITTED.

THAT IS, FOR THOSE WHO BROUGHT THEIR OWN WEAPONRY.

THERE IS NO SET LIMIT TO THE NUMBER OF BB ROUNDS ONE MAY HAVE. ONE MAY CARRY EXTRA MAGAZINES.

Kido Madoka and Umezu Shigeo: School Rumble's First Couple to Kiss.

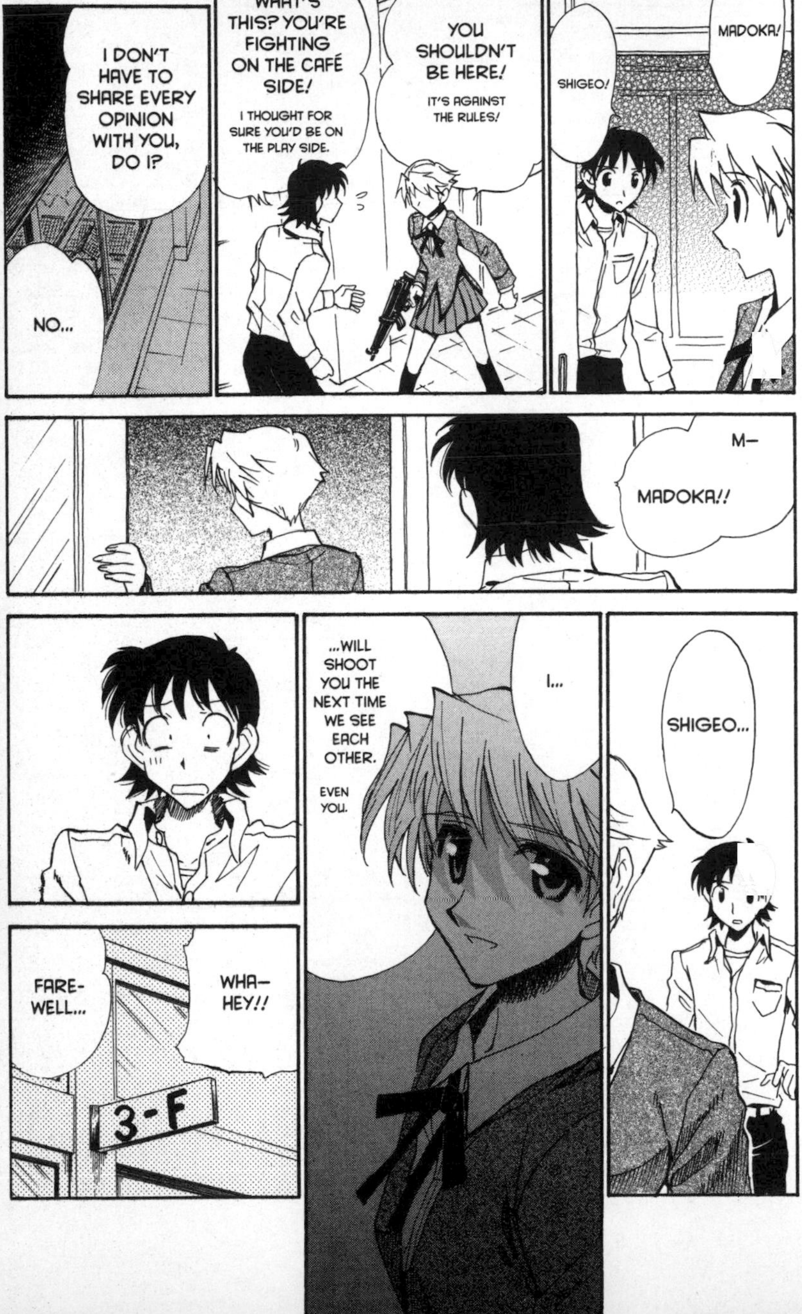
MADOKA!
SHIGEO!
YOU SHOULDN'T BE HERE!
IT'S AGAINST THE RULES!
WHAT'S THIS? YOU'RE FIGHTING ON THE CAFÉ SIDE!
I THOUGHT FOR SURE YOU'D BE ON THE PLAY SIDE.
I DON'T HAVE TO SHARE EVERY OPINION WITH YOU, DO I?
NO...
M—
MADOKA!!
SHIGEO...
I...
...WILL SHOOT YOU THE NEXT TIME WE SEE EACH OTHER.
EVEN YOU.
WHA-HEY!!
FARE-WELL...
3-F

THE MAIN STRENGTH OF THE PLAY ARMY LIES WITH HARIMA... AND WITH SAWACHIKA-KUN.

ANY GOOD BATTLE STRATEGY BEGINS WITH ANALYZING THE ENEMY.

THERE'S ALSO IMADORI.

HE COULD BE CALLED A WEAKNESS.

...WHERE ARE THEY GOING TO ATTACK WITH THE GREATEST STRENGTH?

WE'RE ON THE 4TH FLOOR. THE ENEMY'S ON THE 2ND FLOOR. THE QUESTION IS...

AND HARIMA-KUN LOOKS LIKE HE HAS SOME SKILLS.

DID YOU MAKE YOUR FARE-WELLS TO UMEZU-KUN?

I GUESS.

AHH! SAWACHIKA'S GOTTEN GREEDY AGAIN!

SHE'S JUST THE TYPE TO WIN AT ALL COSTS.

3-F

4F
3F
2F
1F

1-A

WE COULD GET OVERRUN ALL AT ONCE.

NO. IF THE ENEMY CONCENTRATES AT ONE SINGLE POINT, THEY'LL GET THROUGH OUR DEFENSES EASILY.

LOOKING AT OUR BATTLE STRENGTH, DO YOU THINK WE'RE EVENLY MATCHED?

SO WE SHOULD SPREAD OUR FORCES ON ALL THE FLOORS AND SEE HOW THE ENEMY MOVES.

THAT WOULD MAKE THE OTHER FLOORS VERY DANGEROUS.

IF THAT'S TRUE, WE SHOULD CONCEN-TRATE ALL OUR FORCES ON ONE FLOOR.

Playing Tricks on the Leaders Has Also Been Revived.

School Rumble.

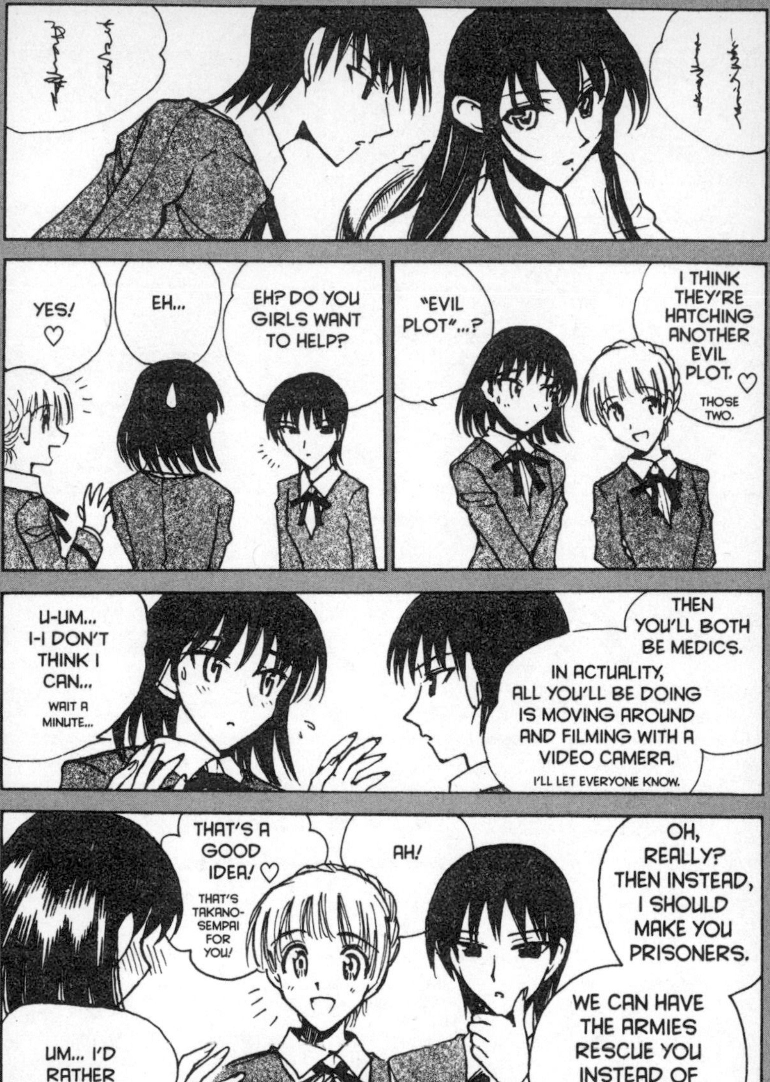
I THINK THEY'RE HATCHING ANOTHER EVIL PLOT. ♡
THOSE TWO.
"EVIL PLOT"...?
EH? DO YOU GIRLS WANT TO HELP?
EH...
YES! ♡
THEN YOU'LL BOTH BE MEDICS.
IN ACTUALITY, ALL YOU'LL BE DOING IS MOVING AROUND AND FILMING WITH A VIDEO CAMERA.
I'LL LET EVERYONE KNOW.
U-UM... I-I DON'T THINK I CAN...
WAIT A MINUTE...
OH, REALLY? THEN INSTEAD, I SHOULD MAKE YOU PRISONERS.
WE CAN HAVE THE ARMIES RESCUE YOU INSTEAD OF CAPTURING THE FLAG...
AH!
THAT'S A GOOD IDEA! ♡
THAT'S TAKANO-SEMPAI FOR YOU!
UM... I'D RATHER BE A MEDIC.

Original Bonus Manga Number 2

#104 THE ULTIMATE THRILL

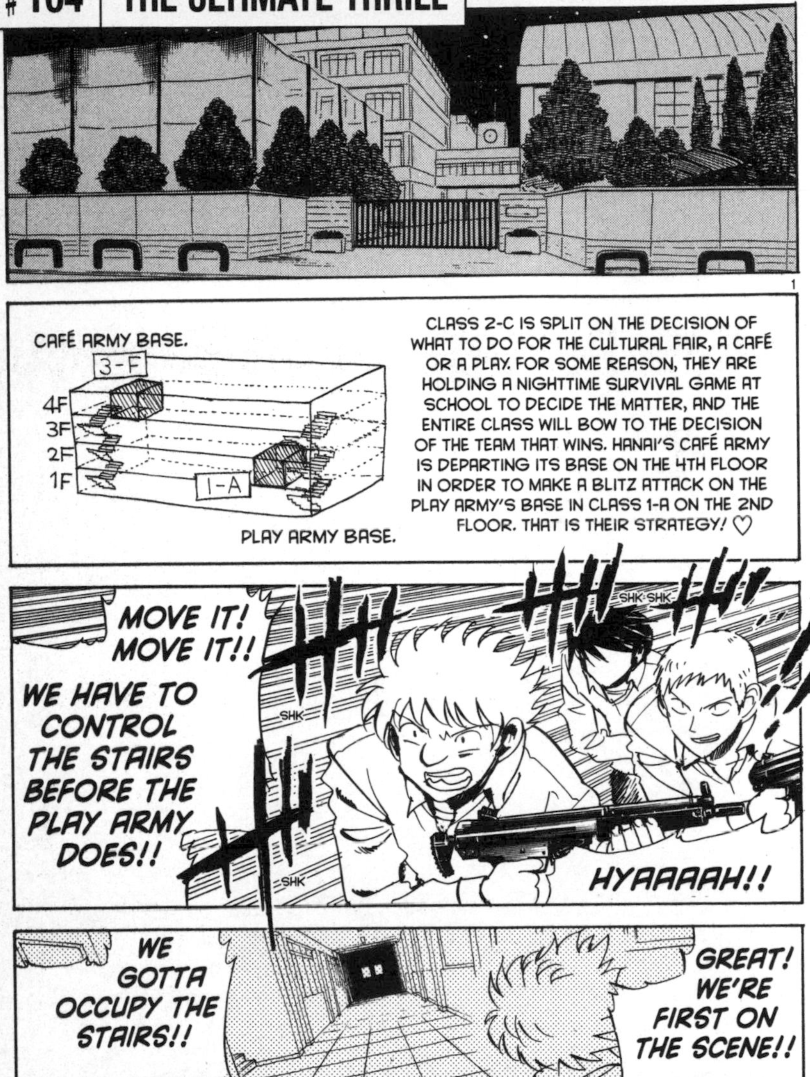
1
CLASS 2-C IS SPLIT ON THE DECISION OF WHAT TO DO FOR THE CULTURAL FAIR, A CAFÉ OR A PLAY. FOR SOME REASON, THEY ARE HOLDING A NIGHTTIME SURVIVAL GAME AT SCHOOL TO DECIDE THE MATTER, AND THE ENTIRE CLASS WILL BOW TO THE DECISION OF THE TEAM THAT WINS. HANAI'S CAFÉ ARMY IS DEPARTING ITS BASE ON THE 4TH FLOOR IN ORDER TO MAKE A BLITZ ATTACK ON THE PLAY ARMY'S BASE IN CLASS 1-A ON THE 2ND FLOOR. THAT IS THEIR STRATEGY! ♡
CAFÉ ARMY BASE.
3-F
4F
3F
2F
1F
1-A
PLAY ARMY BASE.
SHK SHK
HYAAAAH!!
MOVE IT! MOVE IT!!
WE HAVE TO CONTROL THE STAIRS BEFORE THE PLAY ARMY DOES!!
SHK
SHK
GREAT! WE'RE FIRST ON THE SCENE!!
NOW, INTO THE STAIR-WELL!!
WE GOTTA OCCUPY THE STAIRS!!
WE JUST HAVE TO MAKE IT ON TIME...

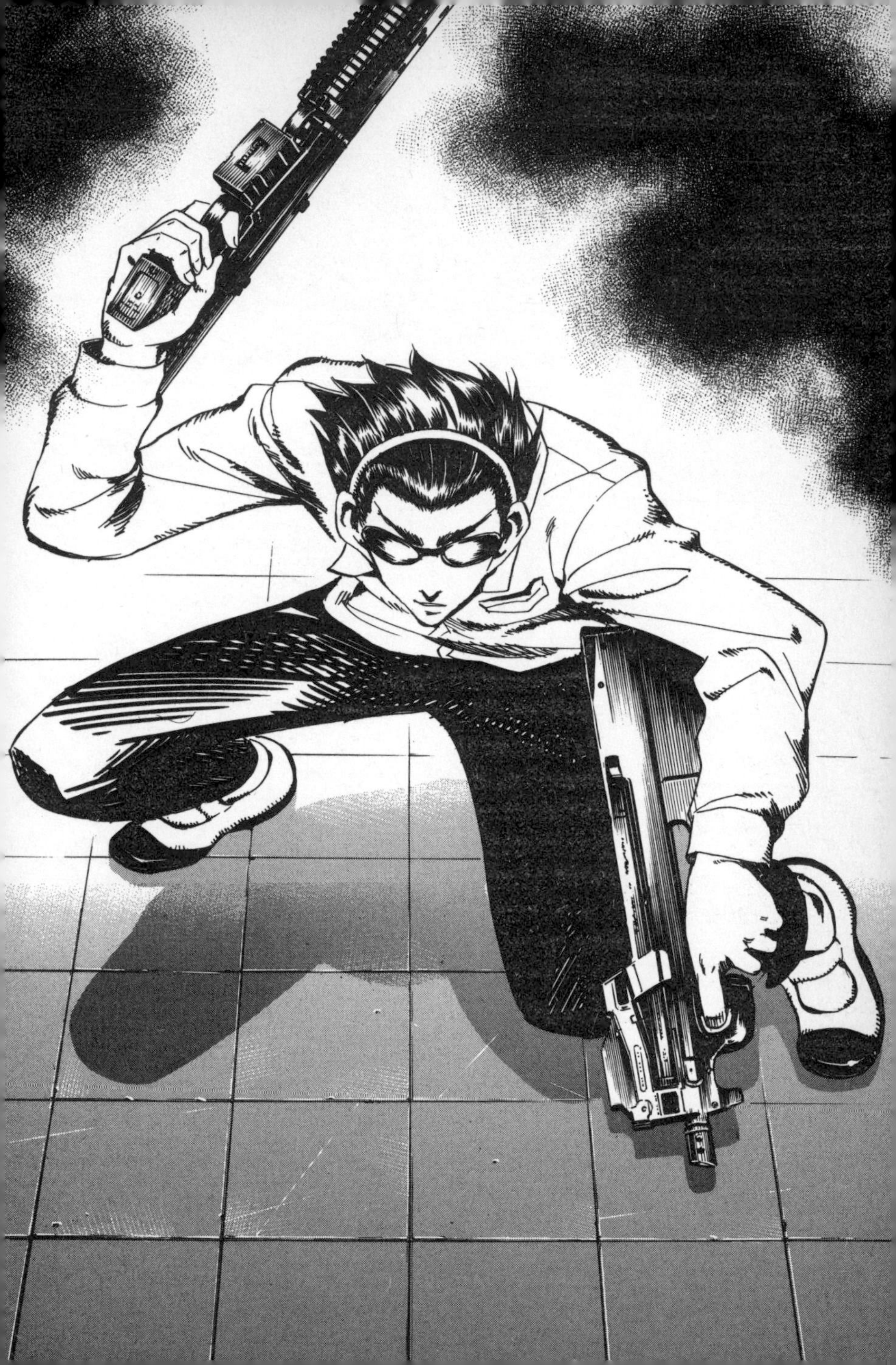

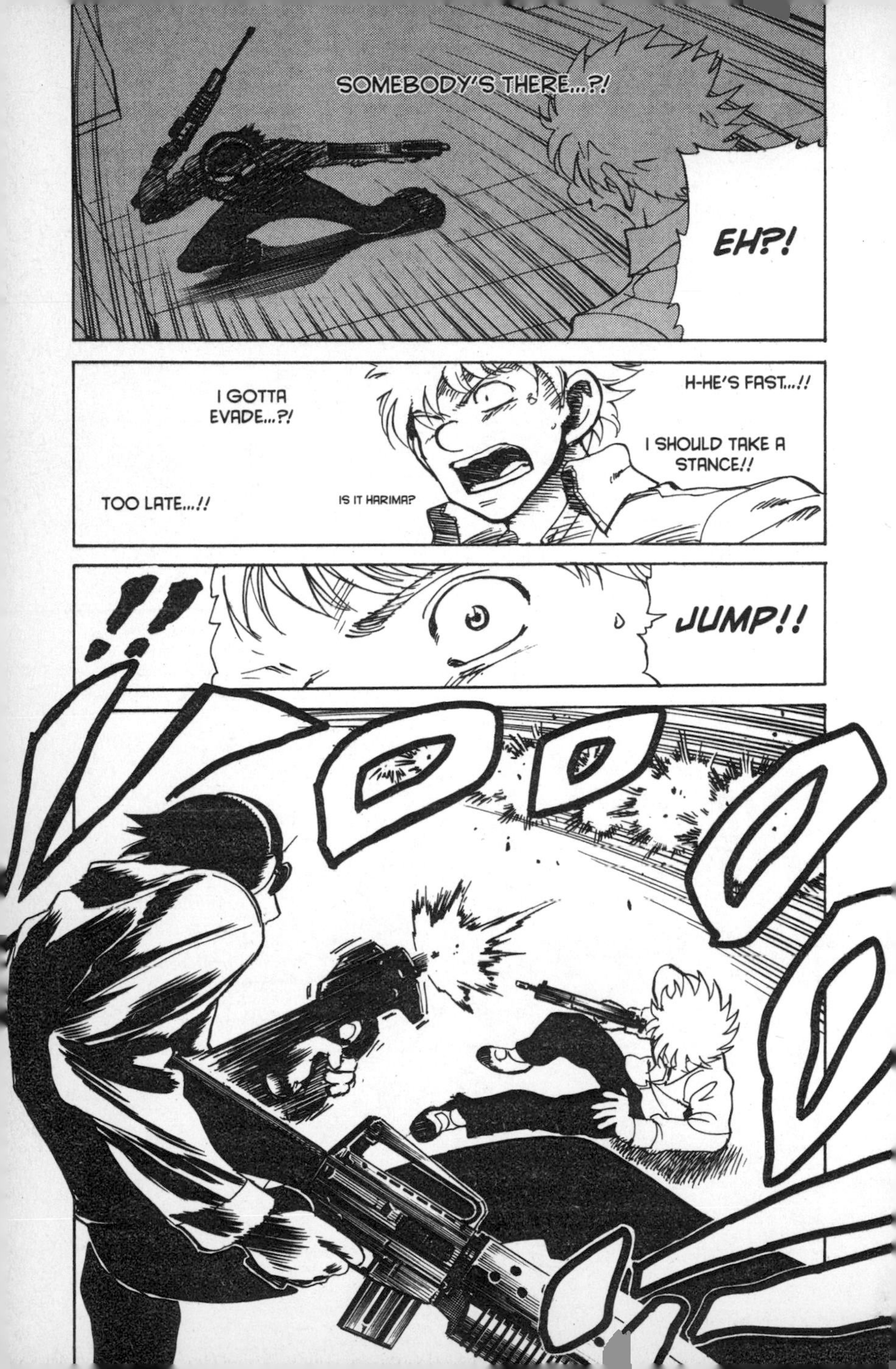
SOMEBODY'S THERE...?!
EH?!
H-HE'S FAST...!!
I SHOULD TAKE A STANCE!!
I GOTTA EVADE...?!
IS IT HARIMA?
TOO LATE...!!
JUMP!!
!!

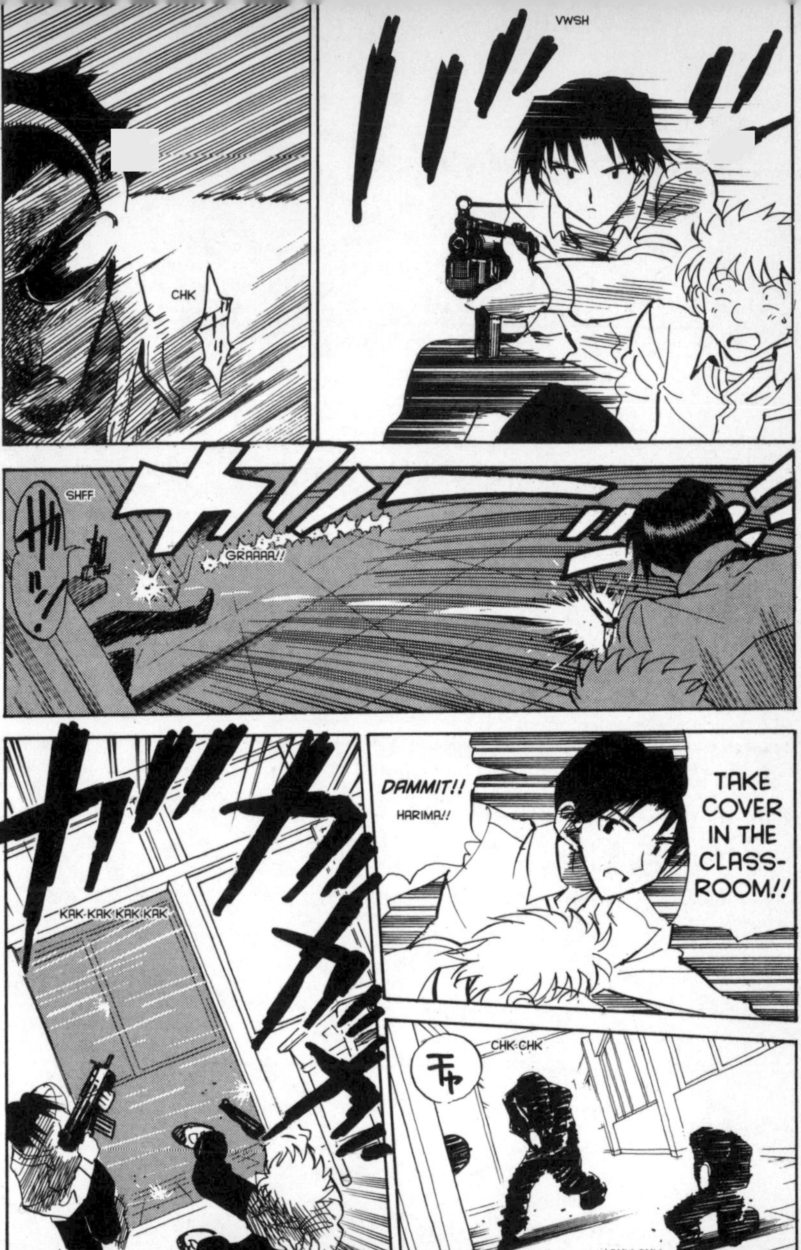
VWSH
CHK
GRAAAA!!
SHFF
TAKE COVER IN THE CLASS-ROOM!!
DAMMIT!!
HARIMA!!
CHK CHK
CHK CHK
KAK KAK KAK KAK

School Rumble.

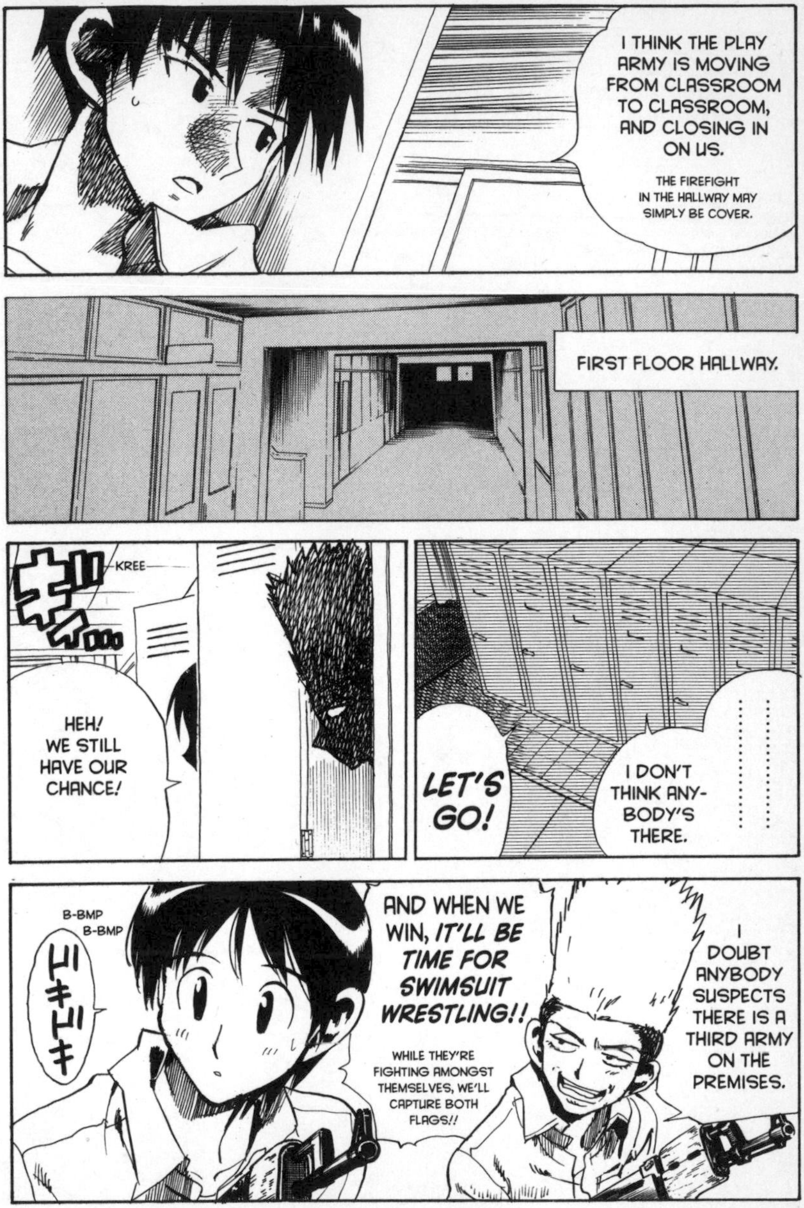
I THINK THE PLAY ARMY IS MOVING FROM CLASSROOM TO CLASSROOM, AND CLOSING IN ON US.
THE FIREFIGHT IN THE HALLWAY MAY SIMPLY BE COVER.
FIRST FLOOR HALLWAY.
......
I DON'T THINK ANY-BODY'S THERE.
LET'S GO!
KREE
HEH! WE STILL HAVE OUR CHANCE!
I DOUBT ANYBODY SUSPECTS THERE IS A THIRD ARMY ON THE PREMISES.
AND WHEN WE WIN, *IT'LL BE TIME FOR SWIMSUIT WRESTLING!!*
WHILE THEY'RE FIGHTING AMONGST THEMSELVES, WE'LL CAPTURE BOTH FLAGS!!
B-BMP B-BMP

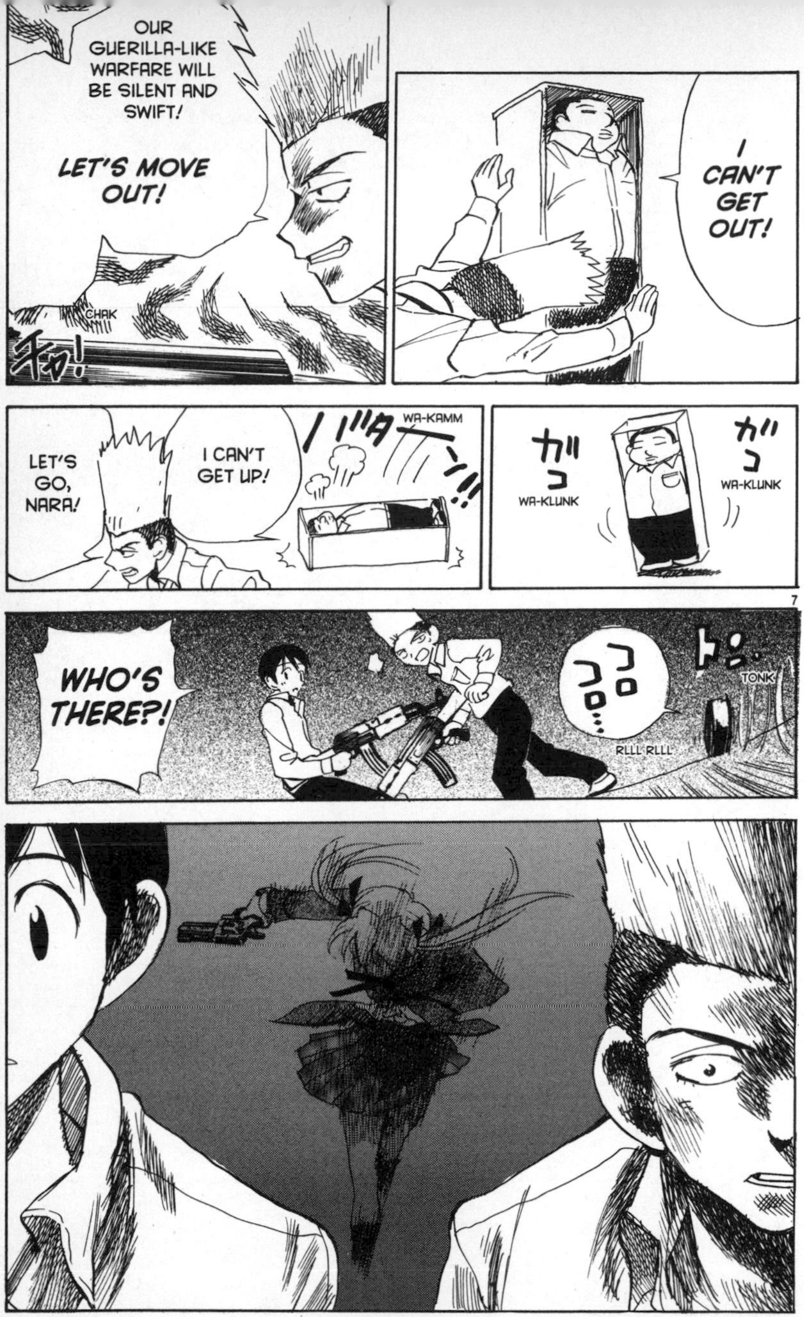
I CAN'T GET OUT!
OUR GUERILLA-LIKE WARFARE WILL BE SILENT AND SWIFT!
LET'S MOVE OUT!
チャ!
CHAK
ガッコ
WA-KLUNK
ガッコ
WA-KLUNK
バターン!!
WA-KAMM
I CAN'T GET UP!
LET'S GO, NARA!
トン。
TONK
コロコロ...
RLLL RLLL
WHO'S THERE?!

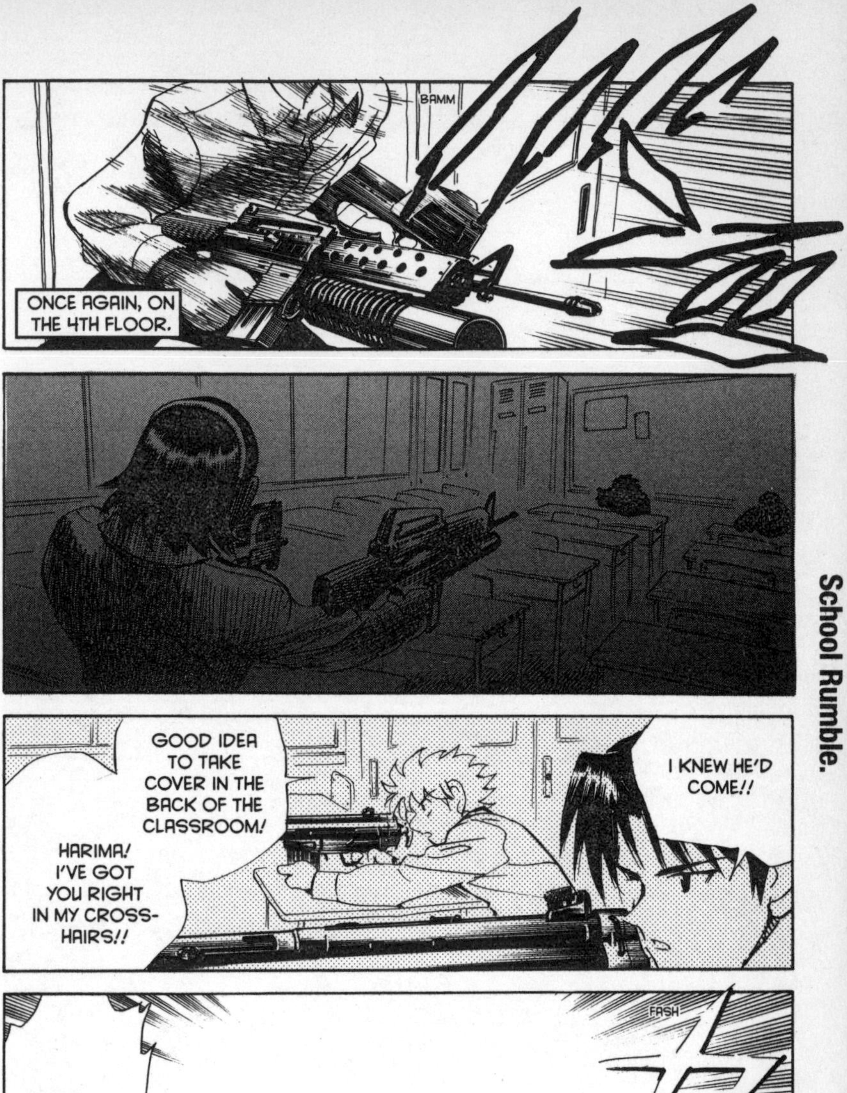
BAMM
ONCE AGAIN, ON THE 4TH FLOOR.
I KNEW HE'D COME!!
GOOD IDEA TO TAKE COVER IN THE BACK OF THE CLASSROOM!
HARIMA! I'VE GOT YOU RIGHT IN MY CROSS-HAIRS!!
FASH
?!

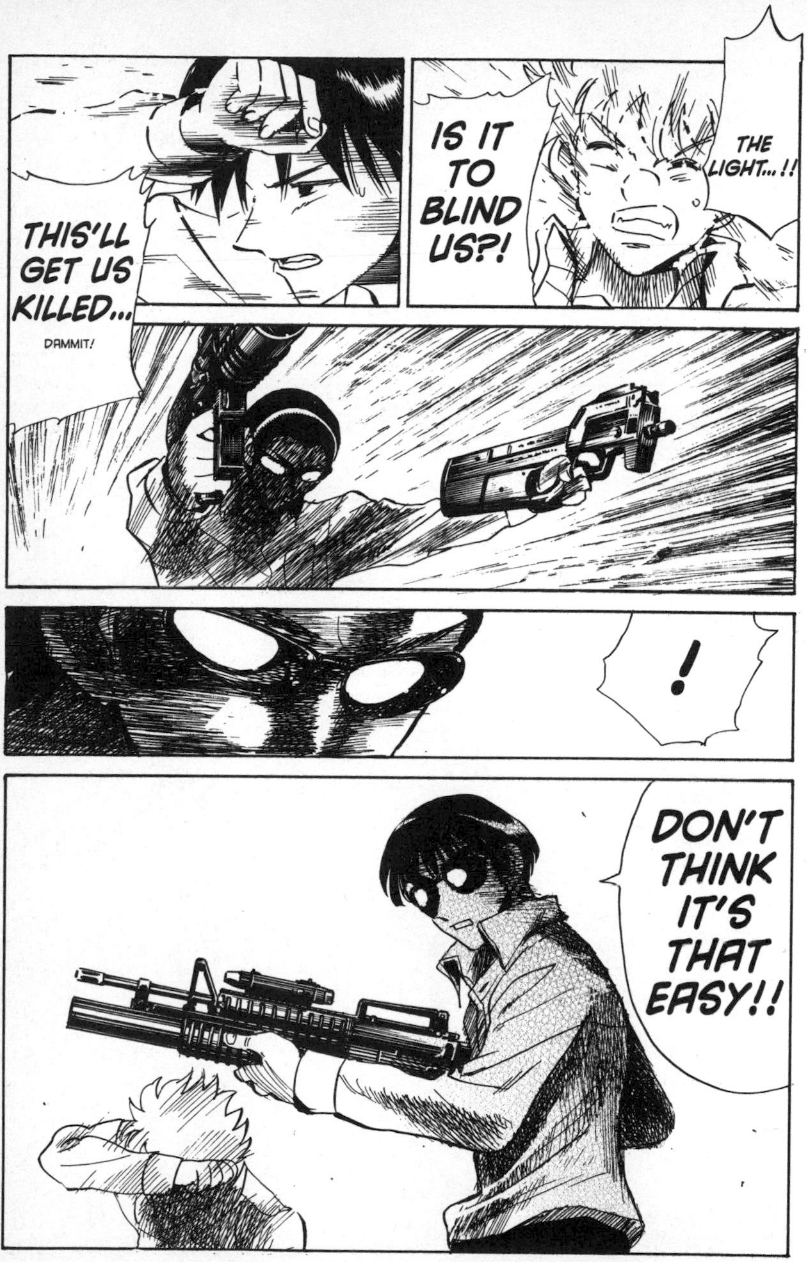
THE LIGHT...!!
IS IT TO BLIND US?!
THIS'LL GET US KILLED...
DAMMIT!
!
DON'T THINK IT'S THAT EASY!!

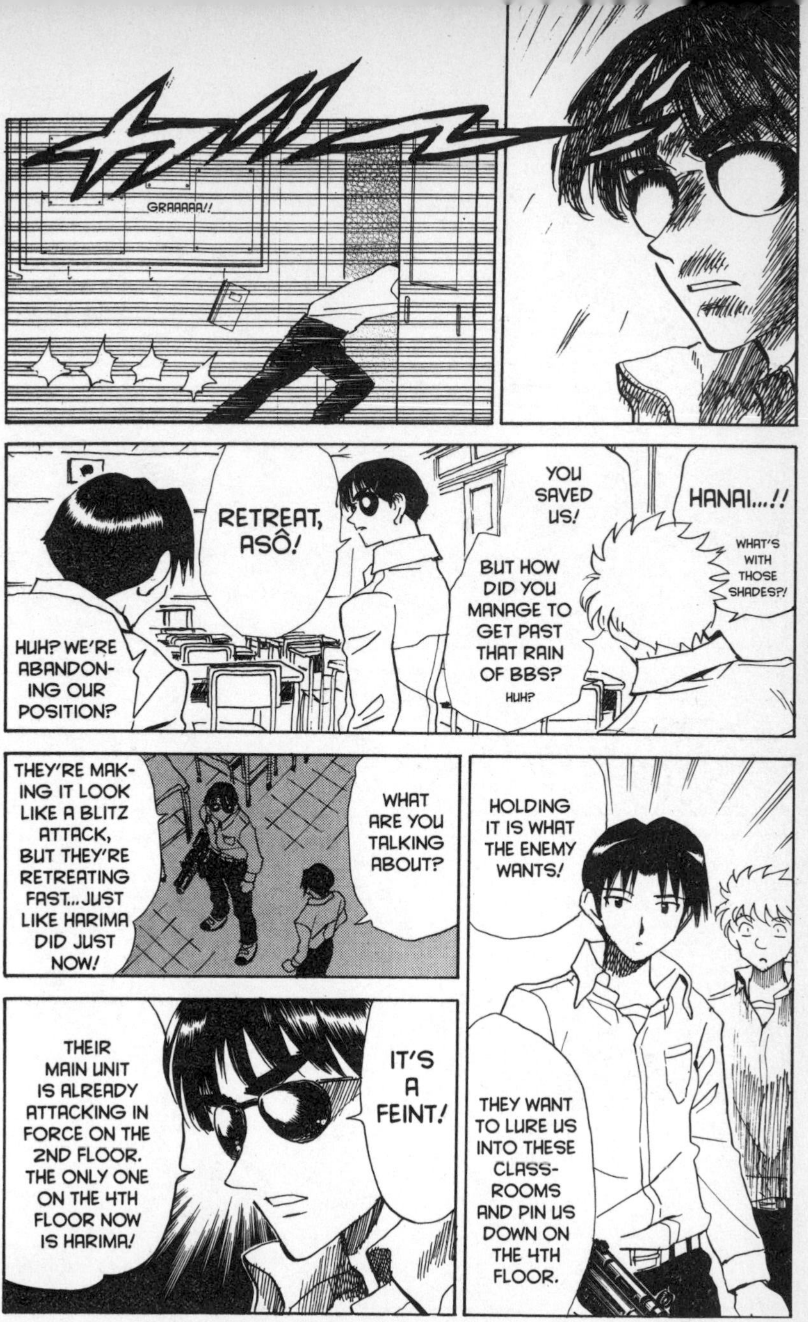
GRAAAAA!!
HANAI...!!
WHAT'S WITH THOSE SHADES?!
YOU SAVED US!
BUT HOW DID YOU MANAGE TO GET PAST THAT RAIN OF BBS?
HUH?
RETREAT, ASÔ!
HUH? WE'RE ABANDON-ING OUR POSITION?
HOLDING IT IS WHAT THE ENEMY WANTS!
THEY WANT TO LURE US INTO THESE CLASS-ROOMS AND PIN US DOWN ON THE 4TH FLOOR.
WHAT ARE YOU TALKING ABOUT?
THEY'RE MAK-ING IT LOOK LIKE A BLITZ ATTACK, BUT THEY'RE RETREATING FAST...JUST LIKE HARIMA DID JUST NOW!
IT'S A FEINT!
THEIR MAIN UNIT IS ALREADY ATTACKING IN FORCE ON THE 2ND FLOOR. THE ONLY ONE ON THE 4TH FLOOR NOW IS HARIMA!

ALSO...

...HE'S PINNING US DOWN WHILE OUR OWN BASE FALLS BEHIND US!

IT'S POSSIBLE THAT WHILE HE'S ATTACK-ING US HERE...

I'M THE ONE TO TAKE DOWN HARIMA!!

WHAT'S HE MEAN BY "OTHER GUY"?!

ROGER!!

NOW! PULL BACK, ASÔ, AND YOU OTHER GUY!!

2ND FLOOR...

WE HAVE TO HOLD OUT UNTIL THEY GET HERE!

THERE'S NOBODY HERE BUT GIRLS!

I'M OUT OF AMMO!

REALLY? TELL THEM TO HURRY!!

IT'S OKAY! ASÔ-KUN'S GROUP WILL BE JOINING US SOON!!

104 ・・・・・・・・ Fin

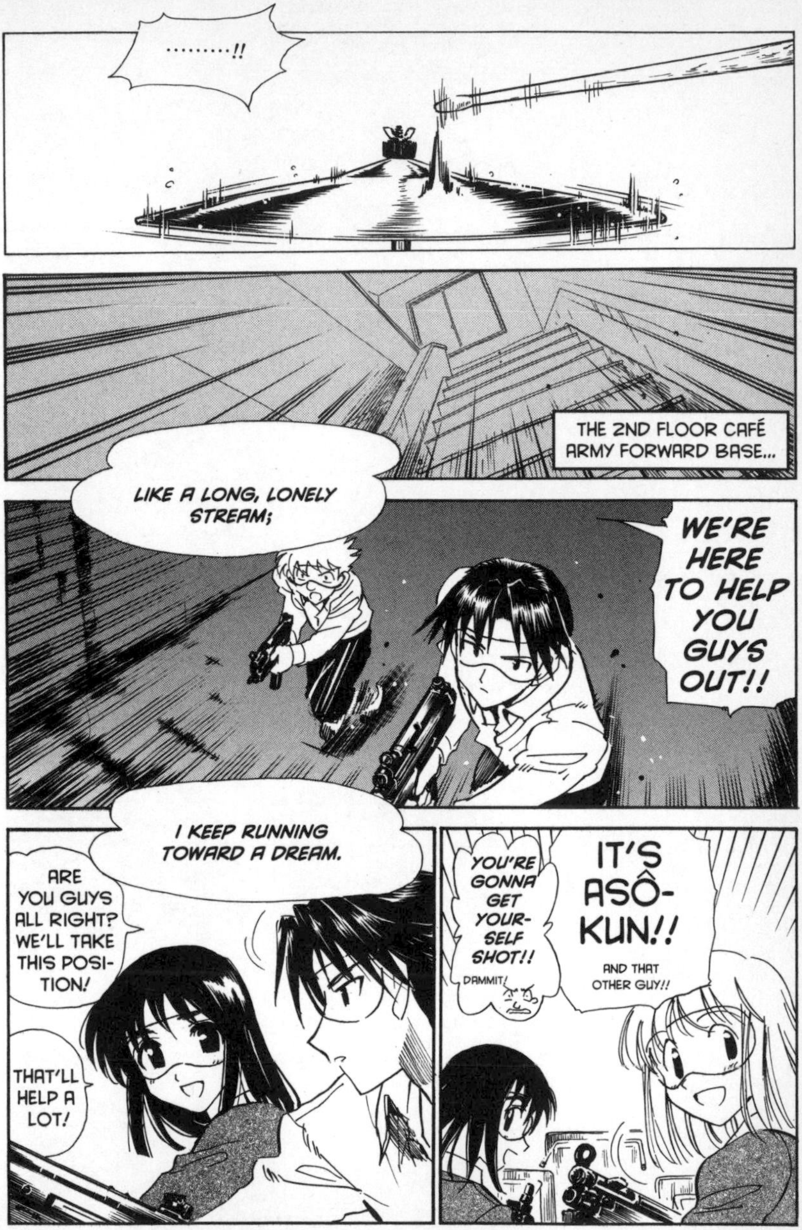
.........!!
THE 2ND FLOOR CAFÉ ARMY FORWARD BASE...
LIKE A LONG, LONELY STREAM;
WE'RE HERE TO HELP YOU GUYS OUT!!
IT'S ASÔ-KUN!!
YOU'RE GONNA GET YOURSELF SHOT!!
DAMMIT!
AND THAT OTHER GUY!!
I KEEP RUNNING TOWARD A DREAM.
ARE YOU GUYS ALL RIGHT? WE'LL TAKE THIS POSITION!
THAT'LL HELP A LOT!

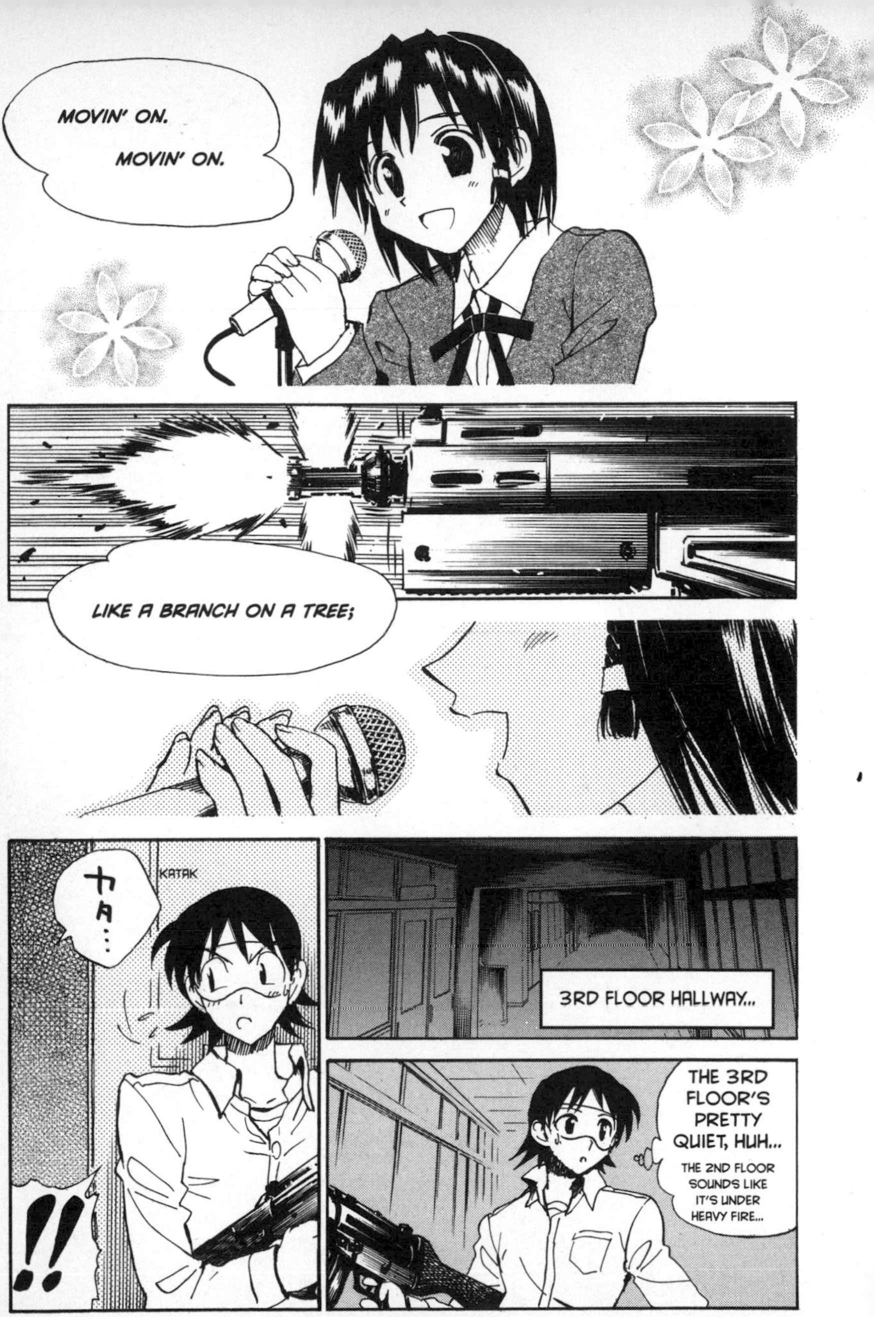
MOVIN' ON.
MOVIN' ON.
LIKE A BRANCH ON A TREE;
3RD FLOOR HALLWAY...
THE 3RD FLOOR'S PRETTY QUIET, HUH...
THE 2ND FLOOR SOUNDS LIKE IT'S UNDER HEAVY FIRE...
KATAK
YA...
!!

The Woman Threw Love Away.

— 91 —

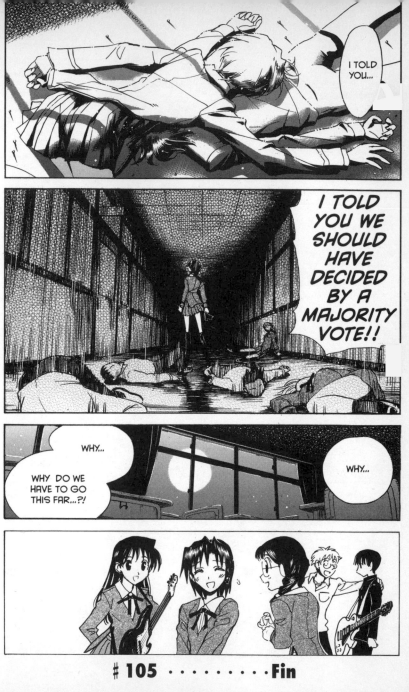

#106 | LA TRAVESTIE

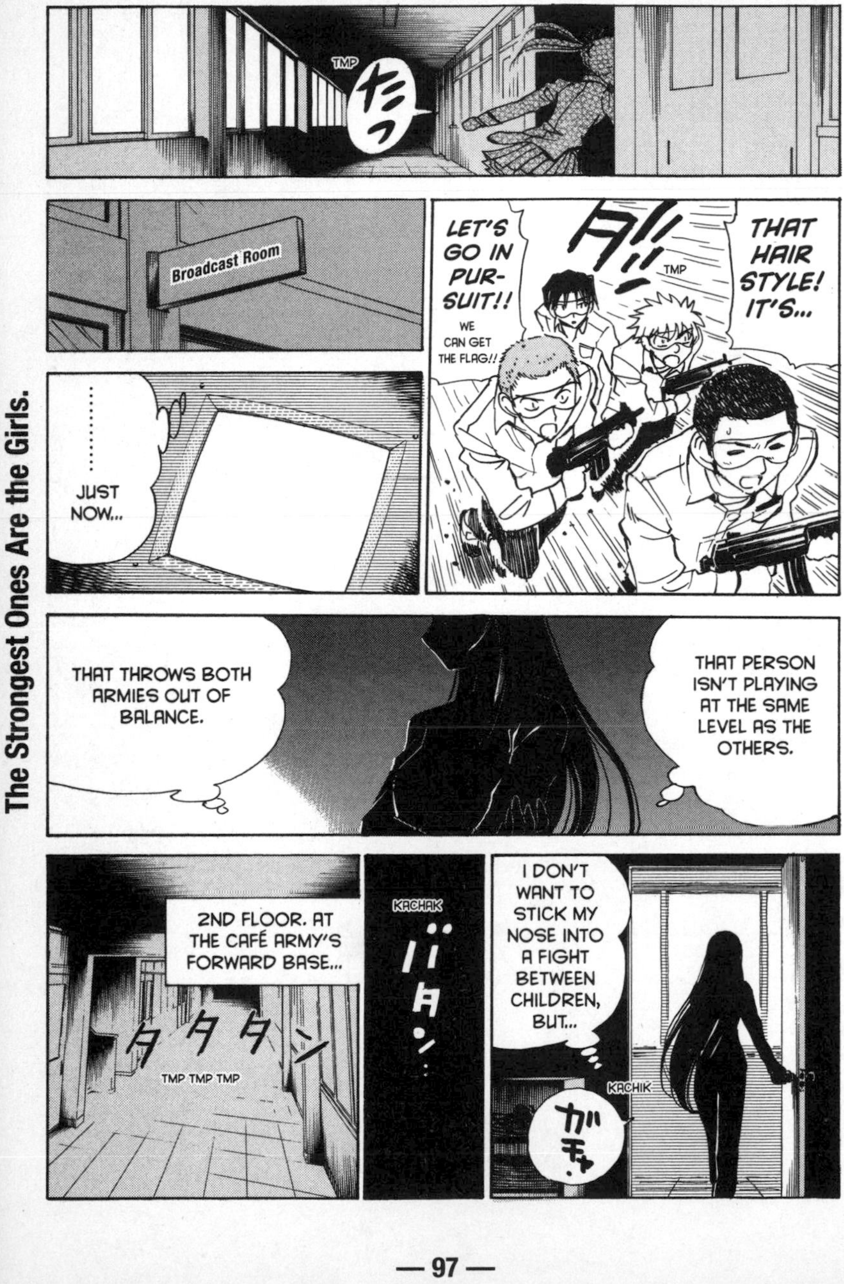
TMP
たっ
THAT HAIR STYLE! IT'S...
LET'S GO IN PURSUIT!!
WE CAN GET THE FLAG!!
タッ!!
TMP
Broadcast Room
......
JUST NOW...
THAT PERSON ISN'T PLAYING AT THE SAME LEVEL AS THE OTHERS.
THAT THROWS BOTH ARMIES OUT OF BALANCE.
I DON'T WANT TO STICK MY NOSE INTO A FIGHT BETWEEN CHILDREN, BUT...
KACHIK
ガチャ
KACHAK
バタン
2ND FLOOR. AT THE CAFÉ ARMY'S FORWARD BASE...
タタタン
TMP TMP TMP

Suô Mikoto: Another Goddess of War.

Misawa: A Drama Fan.

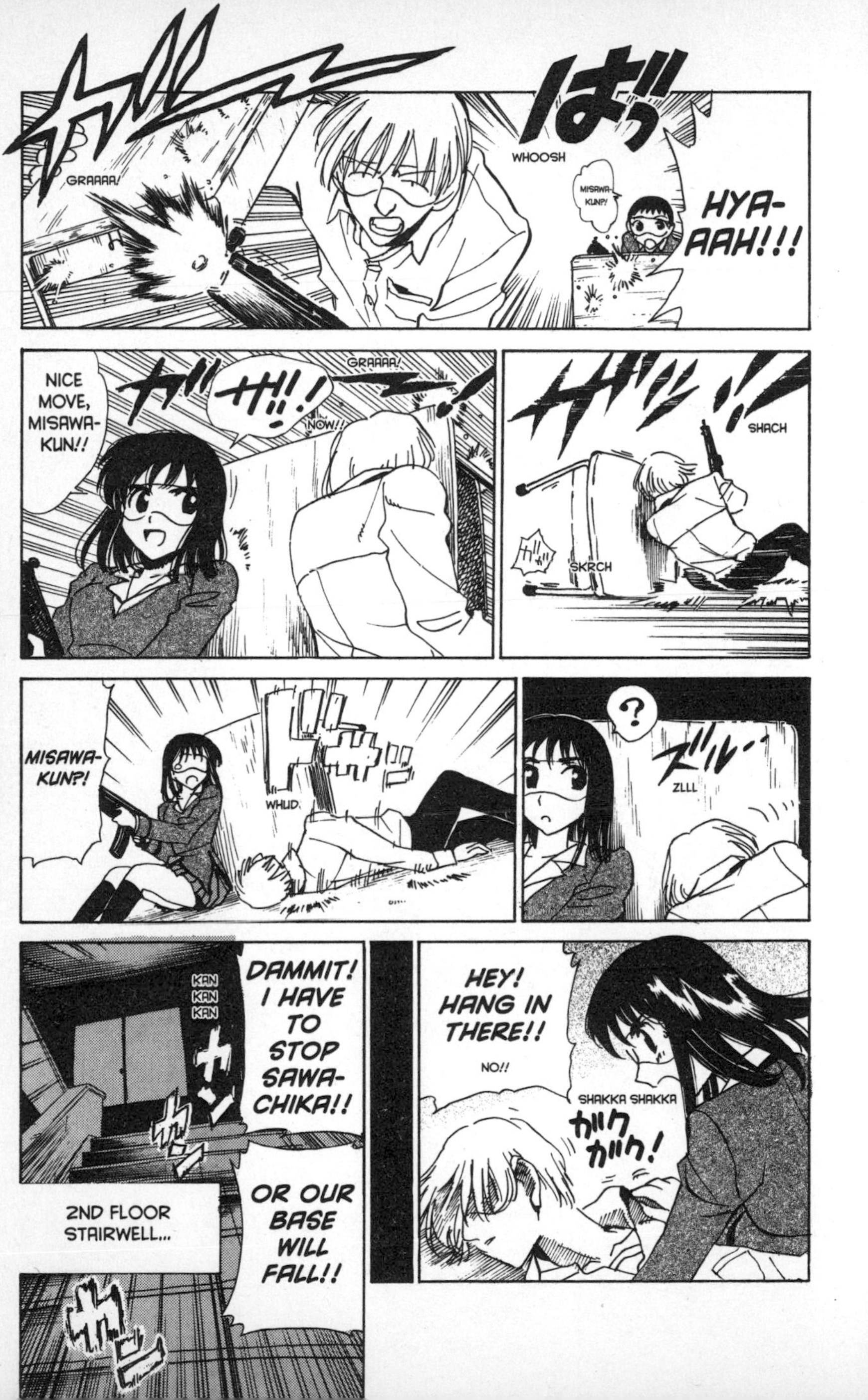
HYA-AAH!!!
MISAWA-KUN?!
WHOOSH
GRAAAA!
SHACH
SKRCH
GRAAAA!
NOW!!
NICE MOVE, MISAWA-KUN!!
?
ZLLL
WHUD
MISAWA-KUN?!
HEY! HANG IN THERE!!
NO!!
SHAKKA SHAKKA
KAN KAN KAN
DAMMIT! I HAVE TO STOP SAWA-CHIKA!!
2ND FLOOR STAIRWELL...
OR OUR BASE WILL FALL!!

Unseen Enemy.

OUR PINCER MOVE ENDED IN FAILURE!!

DAMMIT, WE LOST ANOTHER TWO!!

SAWACHIKA IS TOO GOOD FOR THAT!

SOMETHING IS ODD! SHE SHOWED TOO MUCH OF HERSELF BACK THERE. IS SHE TRYING TO LURE US INTO A TRAP?

BUT... I LIKE OUR CHANCES! IT LOOKS LIKE WE CAN FOLLOW HER MOVEMENTS!

2 - C

PEEP

SHE'S ENTERED CLASS 2-C!

RIGHT! WE'LL FINISH IT OFF HERE. LET'S GO, ASÔ!

TMP-TMP-

たたっ

GO!!

NOW!!

WHOOSH

HUSSSH

カラ…

SHUMP

AND NOW YOU GET YOUR REWARD!

Sawachika Eri: 16 Years Old. Somewhat Rugged Features.

WHO'S THAT?

Only Eight of the Café Army Survive!!

#106 · · · · · · · · · Fin

ZWARA

TSK!

....You May Be One, Too.

BAMM

IF MY NIGHT-VISION SCOPE WERE IN PERFECT SHAPE, I'D HAVE TAKEN HIM OUT WITH ONE SHOT.

THIS IS WHAT I GET FOR USING TOYS.

BUT THAT GUY HAS UNUSUAL MOVES FOR YOUR AVERAGE PERVERT.

TMP

Forgive The Late Introduction. Nakamura, the Sawachika Household Butler.

— 109 —

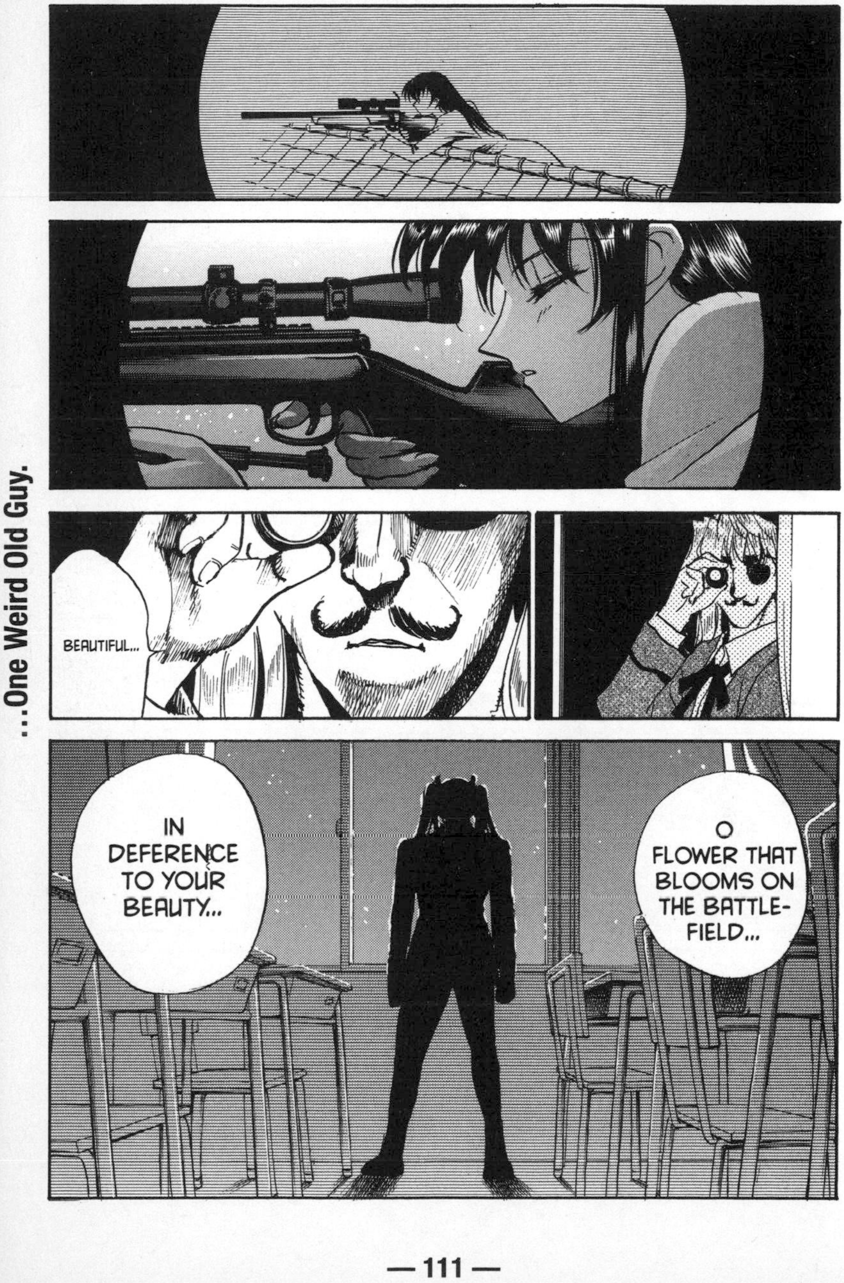
BEAUTIFUL...
O FLOWER THAT BLOOMS ON THE BATTLE-FIELD...
IN DEFERENCE TO YOUR BEAUTY...

Turmoil.

107 · · · · · · · · · Fin

#108 TRULY, MADLY, DEEPLY

CAFE ARMY: HANAI, SUÔ, ASÔ, SUGA.
PLAY ARMY: HARIMA, TSUKAMOTO, SAWACHIKA (THE REAL ONE).
BAND ARMY: KARASUMA, FUYUKI, ICHIJÔ, SAGANO, YÛKI.
NOW, ONLY 12 STUDENTS SURVIVE!!

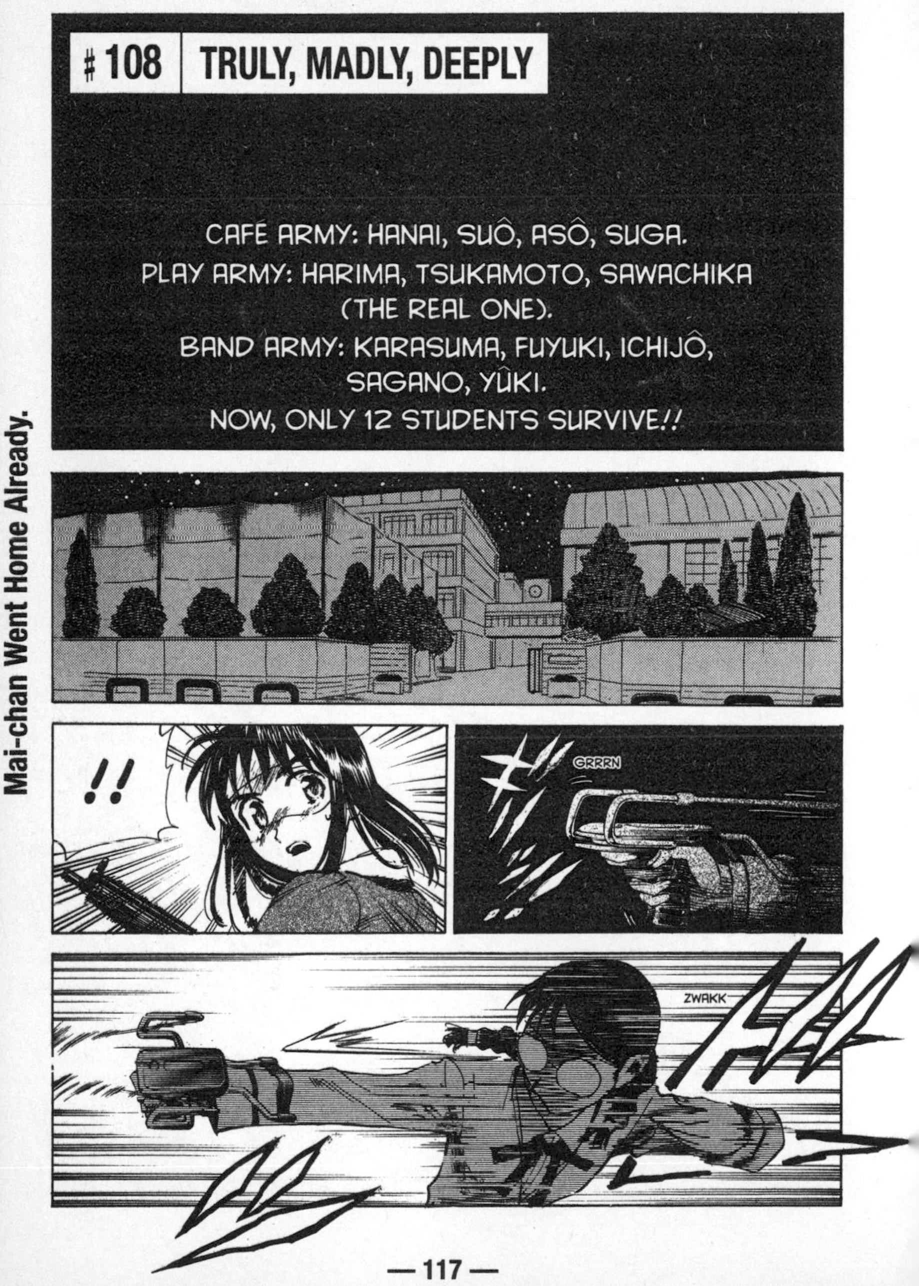
GRRRN
!!
ZWAKK

Mai-chan Went Home Already.

Everything's All Mixed Up.

WE'RE IN THE MIDDLE OF A BATTLE-FIELD HERE!

WAKE UP TO REALITY, HANAI!!

Y-YÛKI-KUN!!

YÛKI-SAN...

I'M SORRY...

ALL RIGHT... LET'S GO.

KH...!!

TMP

Farewell, Tsumugi.

RIGHT!!

WE HAVE TO TAKE DOWN THE BAND ARMY BEFORE THEY CAPTURE OUR FLAG! LET'S GO!!

SHKK

WHAT'S THAT?! THE BAND MEMBERS?!

The Battle's Climax.

DON'T SWEAT IT! WE'RE FAR BETTER WAR-RIORS THAN ANY OF THEM!!

WE'LL HEAD UP TO CARRY OFF THE CAFÉ ARMY FLAG TO SAFETY!!

GOT IT! JUST LEAVE IT TO US! WE'LL PROTECT THE FLAG!

WH-WHAT THE—!?

!!

SUGA! LOOK!

— 121 —

Also Known As: That Other Guy.

BLAMM

COME IN!!

CHK

ZZT

WHAT?!
WHAT
WAS
THAT
NOISE?!
ASÔ?!
SUGA?!

SHF

2ND FLOOR PLAY
ARMY BASE...

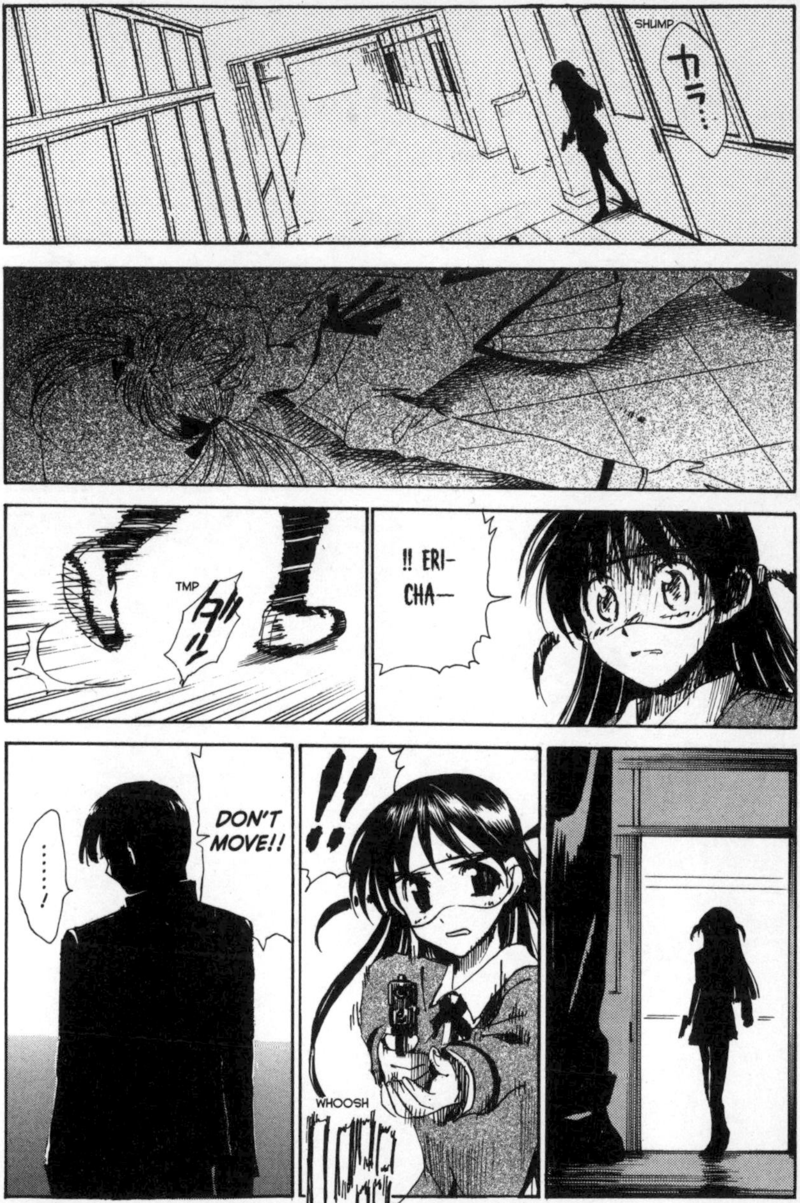
SHUMP
カラ…
!! ERI-CHA—
TMP
タッ
!!
WHOOSH
DON'T MOVE!!
......!

Sawachika Eri: KIA

I WAS AS CAUTIOUS AS POSSIBLE COMING HERE, BUT...

IN THE END I LET MY GUARD DOWN, HUH?

HELLO, TSUKAMOTO-SAN.

THE MOON IS BEAUTIFUL TONIGHT.

WHY ARE YOU EVEN HERE?!

......

WHY? KARASUMA-KUN!

THEY'RE RIGHT IN FRONT OF 3-E.

...CONFIRMED! IT'S SUÔ-SAN AND HANAI.

NEARING THE 4TH FLOOR CAFÉ MAIN BASE.

ROGER!

Y-YEAH...

LET'S PERFORM THE PINCER MOVE JUST AS PLANNED!

THE ENEMY IS PROBABLY PLANNING A COMBINED ATTACK.

NOW... IS THE MOMENT OF TRUTH.

Mighty Warriors Both.

SUÔ, YOU AND I ARE A DEADLY COMBINATION!!

WE'LL BE FINE AS LONG AS YOU'VE GOT MY BACK!

108 .... Fin

♭21 NUIT DOCILE

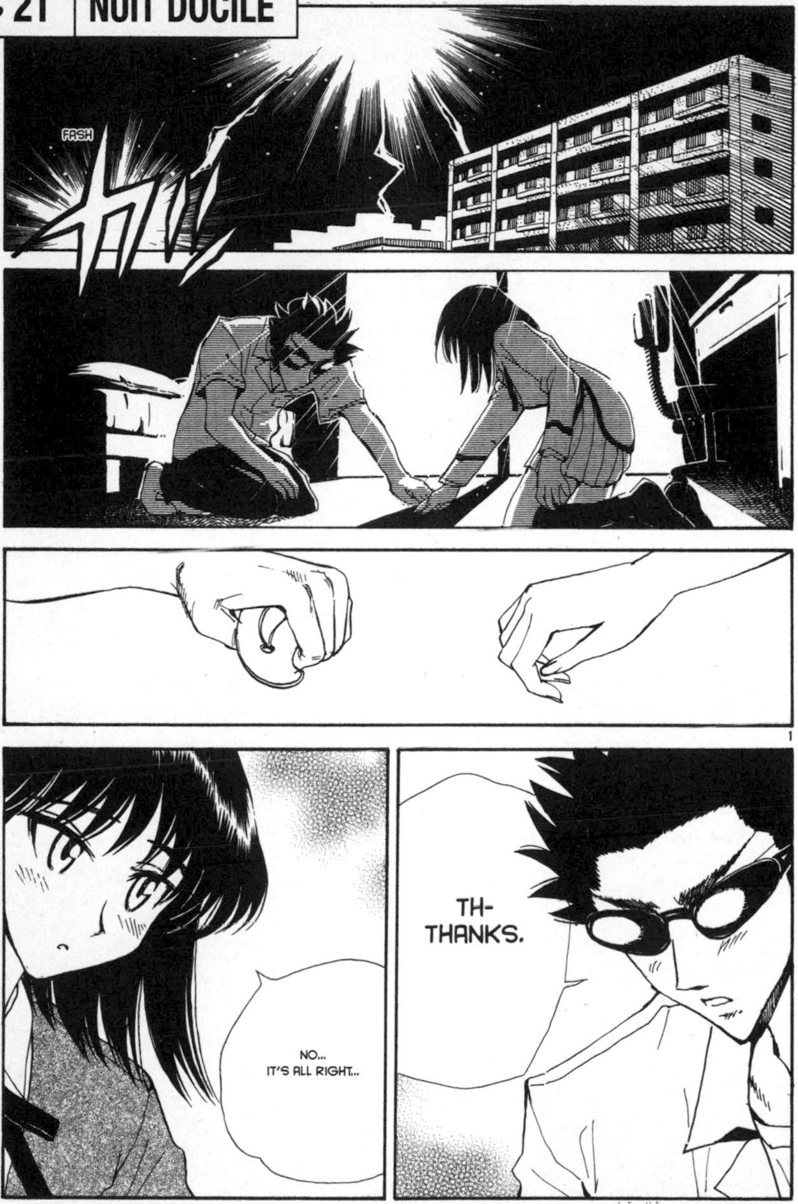
FASH
TH-
THANKS.
NO...
IT'S ALL RIGHT...

The Two Alone in the Dark.

THAT'S IT! JUST THAT LIGHTING!

OH, YEAH... WHILE WE'RE AT IT, COULD YOU READ THE DIALOG FOR THIS SCENE ALOUD? THAT SHOULD GIVE ME AN EVEN MORE SOLID IMAGE.

OKAY...

I COULDN'T COME UP WITH THE IMAGE IN MY MIND, BUT LOOKING AT YOU NOW, I CAN PICTURE IT!

THANKS!

NO, I MEAN... IN THE MANGA, THE HERO AND HEROINE ARE IN A CAVE, AND THERE'S A SCENE WHERE THEY'RE BEING LIT BY A FIRE.

THAT'S IT. THAT'S THE LOOK.

OH...?

THAT'S IT!! THAT'S THE WAY!!

"SO WE'RE FINALLY ALONE TOGETHER ON A DESERT ISLAND, HUH?"

This Story: Bad for the Heart.

— 132 —

Just Then, He Saw Tenma.

♭21・・・・・・・・Fin

WE CAN'T HAVE MORE INJURIES, SO I'LL CLEAN THIS UP.

CHINK

THAT YOSHIDA-YAMA... CAN YOU STAND?

EH? WAIT! MY LENSES...!

SEE YOU.

I GUESS A HIGH-SCHOOL STUDENT WOULD HAVE A HARD TIME BEING NICE ALL OF THE TIME.

FOR PITY'S SAKE! I DON'T KNOW IF HE'S OFFICIOUS OR NOSY, BUT HIS PERSONALITY IS SOMEWHERE IN THAT RANGE.

· · ·

3

DOKAMM

WA!

WA!

AFTER SCHOOL...

I WONDER IF I CAN RIDE A BIKE WITHOUT MY GLASSES...

Hanai Haruki: An Excessively Serious Man.

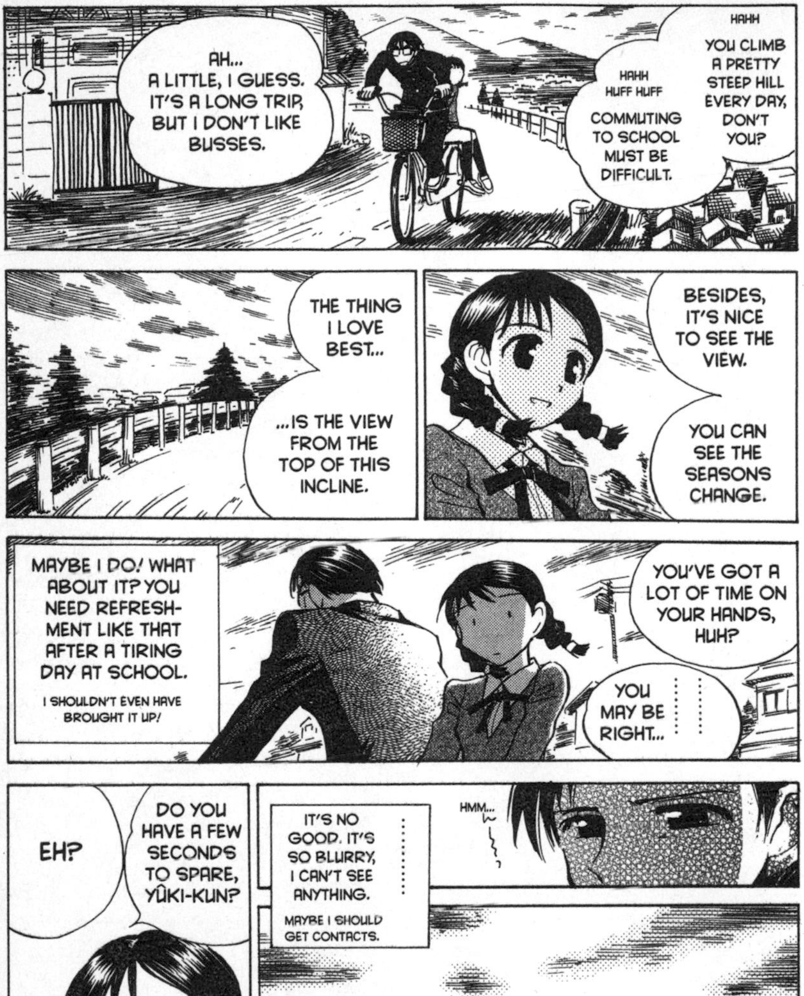
HAHH
YOU CLIMB A PRETTY STEEP HILL EVERY DAY, DON'T YOU?
HAHH HUFF HUFF
COMMUTING TO SCHOOL MUST BE DIFFICULT.
AH... A LITTLE, I GUESS. IT'S A LONG TRIP, BUT I DON'T LIKE BUSSES.
BESIDES, IT'S NICE TO SEE THE VIEW.
YOU CAN SEE THE SEASONS CHANGE.
THE THING I LOVE BEST...
...IS THE VIEW FROM THE TOP OF THIS INCLINE.
YOU'VE GOT A LOT OF TIME ON YOUR HANDS, HUH?
YOU MAY BE RIGHT... ......
MAYBE I DO! WHAT ABOUT IT? YOU NEED REFRESH-MENT LIKE THAT AFTER A TIRING DAY AT SCHOOL.
I SHOULDN'T EVEN HAVE BROUGHT IT UP!
HMM...
IT'S NO GOOD. IT'S SO BLURRY, I CAN'T SEE ANYTHING. ......
MAYBE I SHOULD GET CONTACTS.
DO YOU HAVE A FEW SECONDS TO SPARE, YÛKI-KUN?
EH?

...Is Because He Is Too Nice a Guy.

IT'S A RAINBOW...

I THOUGHT A VIEW LIKE THAT WAS TOO GOOD TO LET PASS BY.

WELL? AREN'T YOU GLAD YOU LOOKED?

REALLY. I JUST DON'T GET IT...

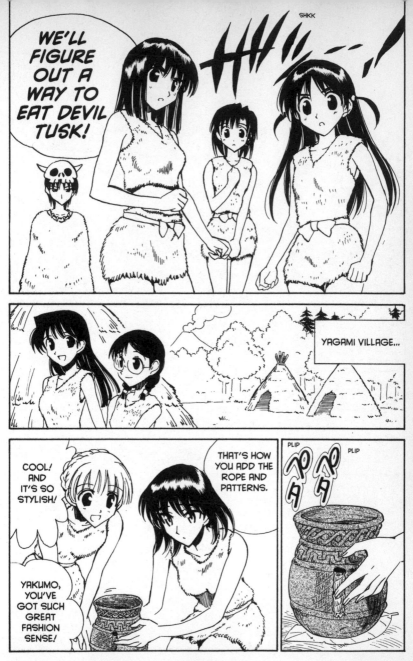

HIT HIM
WITH
THE
BLACK-
ROCK
WEAP-
ONS!!

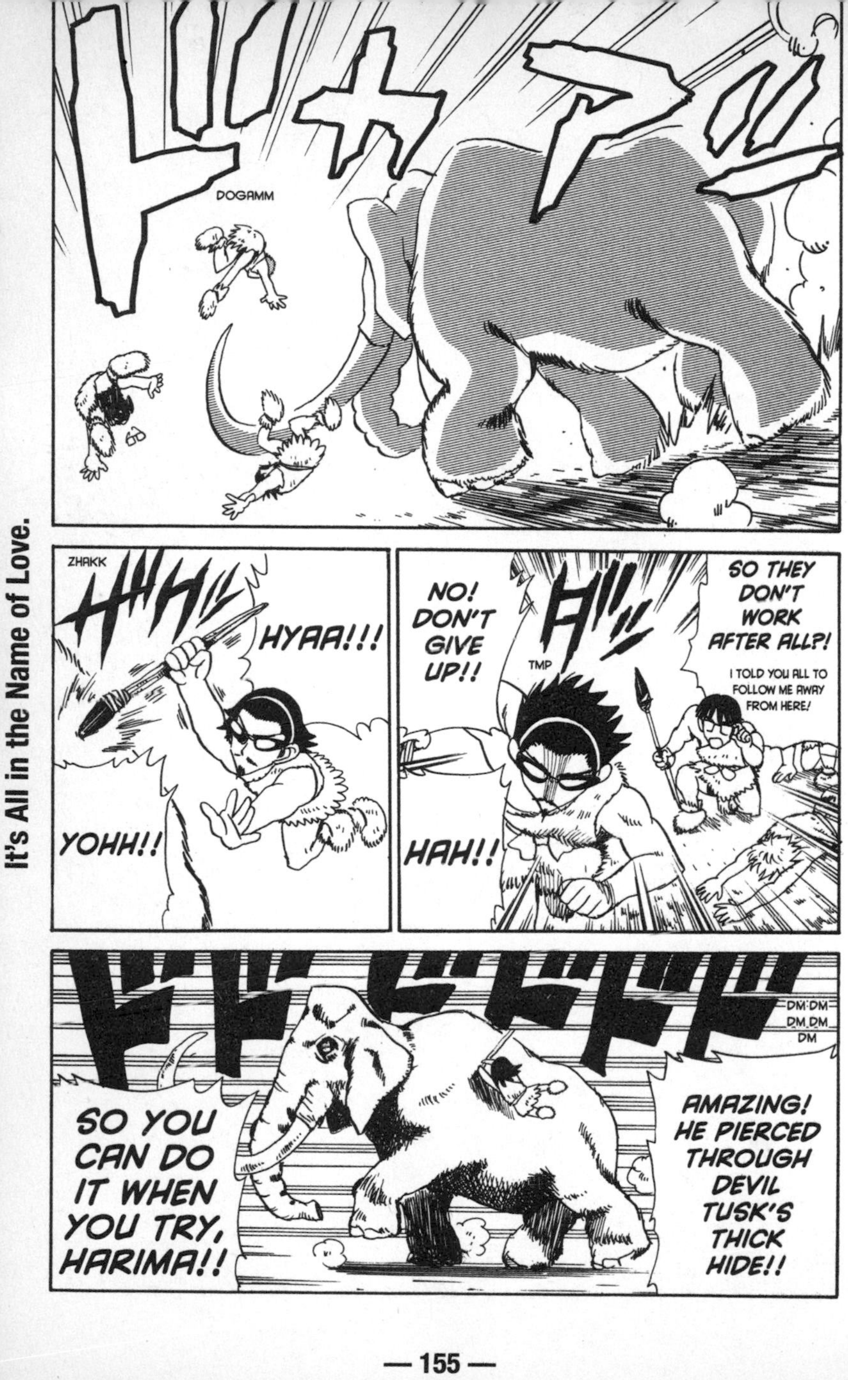
DOGAMM
SO THEY DON'T WORK AFTER ALL?!
I TOLD YOU ALL TO FOLLOW ME AWAY FROM HERE!
NO! DON'T GIVE UP!!
TMP
HAH!!
ZHAKK
HYAA!!!
YOHH!!
DM DM DM DM DM
AMAZING! HE PIERCED THROUGH DEVIL TUSK'S THICK HIDE!!
SO YOU CAN DO IT WHEN YOU TRY, HARIMA!!

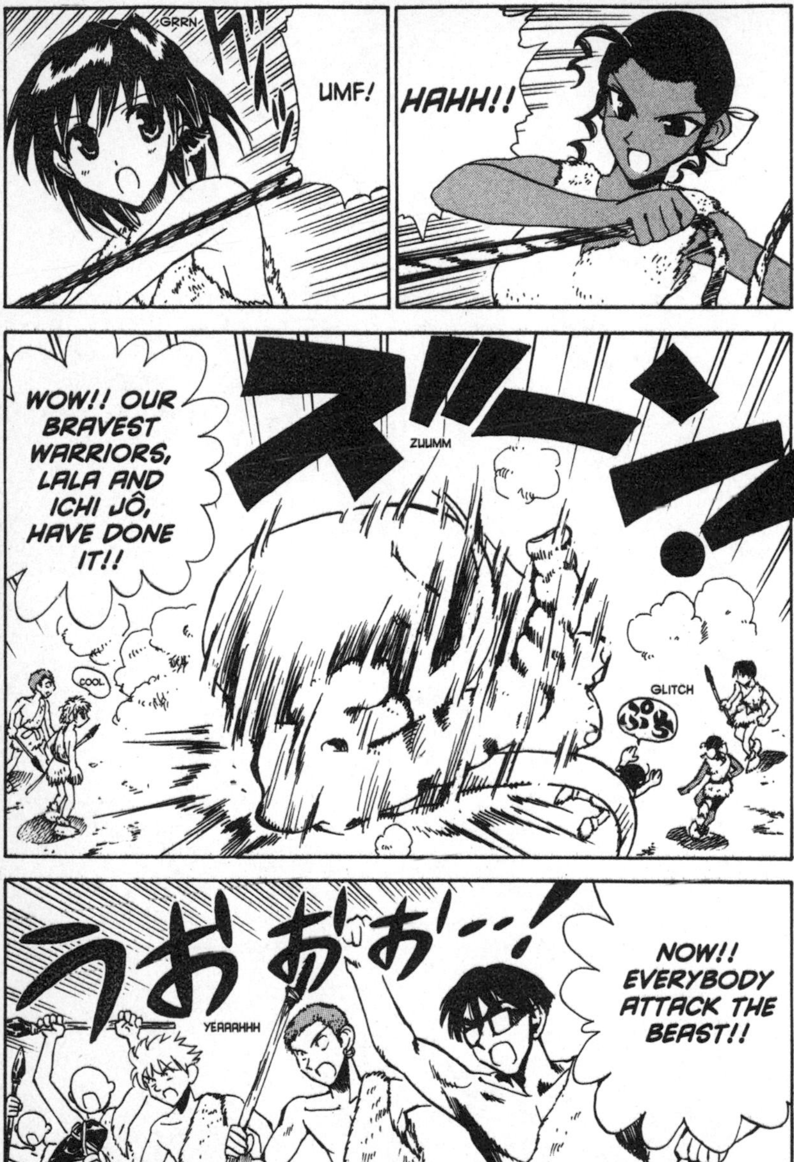
HAHH!!
GRRN
UMF!
ZUUMM
WOW!! OUR BRAVEST WARRIORS, LALA AND ICHI JÔ, HAVE DONE IT!!
GLITCH
COOL
NOW!! EVERYBODY ATTACK THE BEAST!!
YEAAAHHH

Mammoth Snout.

TO LIVE LIKE A TURTLE

By Nijô Jô

THE END

Original Bonus Manga Number 3

About the Creator

Jin Kobayashi was born in Tokyo. *School Rumble* is his first manga series. He has answered these questions from his fans:

What is your hobby?
Basketball

Which manga inspired you to become a creator?
Dragon Ball

Which character in your manga do you like best?
Kenji Harima

What type of manga do you want to create in the future?
Action

Name one book, piece of music, or movie you like.
The Indiana Jones series

Translation Notes

Japanese is a tricky language for most Westerners, and translation is often more art than science. For your edification and reading pleasure, here are notes on some of the places where we could have gone in a different direction in our translation of the work, or where a Japanese cultural reference is used.

Zabuton Cushions, page 6

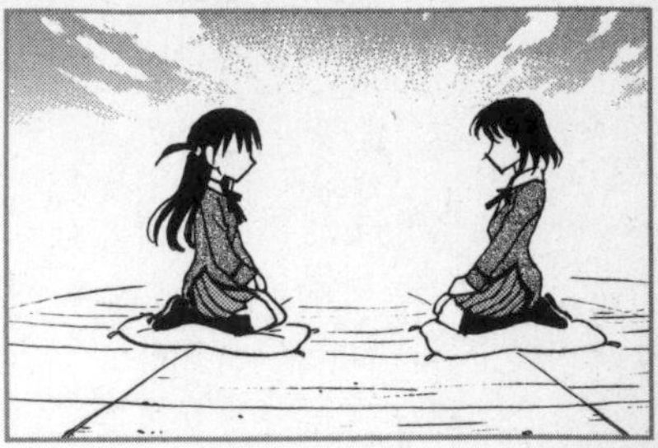

Before most Japanese homes had Western-style furnishings, floors were covered with *tatami* mats. Even now, nearly every home has at least one *tatami* room used for receiving guests, among other purposes. Tatami mats are made of rushes tightly bound into long rectangles. They have a bit of "give" to them so that not a lot of added padding is necessary when sleeping or sitting down. *Zabuton* cushions, about three feet square and two to three inches thick, were made for use on *tatami* mats. Pulling out a *zabuton* when one is to have a serious talk is a part of Japanese culture.

Suke-san, Kaku-san, page 12

A *jidai-geki* called "Mito Kômon" has been running so long, the actor playing the main character has changed four times due to old age. Mito Kômon (whom Tenma resembles in the panel) is an elderly uncle of the Shogun. He and his henchmen wander the land to right injustices caused by ambitious and greedy people. About fifty minutes into each show there is a large brawl, and out comes the Shogun's family seal, proof of Mito Kômon's relationship with the head of state. With that the bad guys bow down, knowing they can't

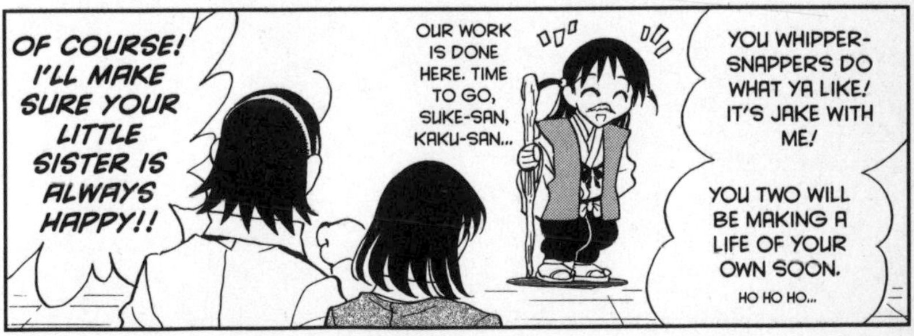
YOU WHIPPER-SNAPPERS DO WHAT YA LIKE! IT'S JAKE WITH ME!
YOU TWO WILL BE MAKING A LIFE OF YOUR OWN SOON.
HO HO HO...
OUR WORK IS DONE HERE. TIME TO GO, SUKE-SAN, KAKU-SAN...
OF COURSE! I'LL MAKE SURE YOUR LITTLE SISTER IS ALWAYS HAPPY!!

stand against the Shogun's power. Although there are quite a few regulars who make up Mito Kômon's little band, the two main loyal servants are Suke and Kaku.

I Just Got Here, page 15

I-I JUST GOT HERE.
PER-FECT JOY!!!
ONE OF THE TOP EIGHT (APPROXIMATELY) THINGS THAT HARIMA HAS ALWAYS WANTED TO SAY TO HIS DATE.
TAN-TAN-TAAA!

The second to arrive for a date will usually apologize for getting there late and ask if the person has been waiting long. No matter how long the wait might have been, the gallant thing to say is *Ima kita tokoro*, which means that he or she got there only a few short minutes before the date did. The phrase appears in romances all the time.

All the Way into Tokyo, page 17

Most of the suburban areas around Tokyo are fully functioning towns unto themselves. Unless suburban residents work in Tokyo, many of them hardly ever travel there. The Tokyo trip is for special occasions such as concerts or other special entertainment, or for shopping for hard-to-find items.

Crepe Shop, page 17

These thin flour pancakes rolled with jam and other fillings have been a hit with Japanese tastebuds since the Meiji Era at the turn of the twentieth century.

Shadow Is Light . . ., page 31

Much like Western students assigned to read Shakespeare, Japanese students must learn and memorize classic Japanese literature. Most of these books are hundreds of years old, and the Japanese language has evolved quite a lot in the intervening years. The present word for "shadow," *kage*, actually refers to the image that light creates, and therefore the word (especially in classic Japanese literature) actually means light rather than darkness. Eri, who is unfamiliar with Japanese word origins, sees the two as opposites.

Cultural Fair, page 43

In addition to the athletics festival, nearly every school also has a cultural fair for which each class, club, team, or other official school group must provide some form of entertainment. Most common are food stalls, but activities also include haunted houses, museum-like displays, puppet shows, music, and dance performances.

Hanafuda, page 49

Did you think that Nintendo started with Donkey Kong? No, Nintendo was in business making a card deck called Hanafuda in the late 1800s. Cards were introduced to Japan in the 1500s, when Portuguese sailors brought their 48-card decks with them to Japan. Card games have been somewhat popular ever since, but during the Edo Period (1603–1868), small cards were created with 12 suits representing the months, each suit having four cards imprinted with the image of a flower that matches the month. Because the cards (*fuda*) are printed with flowers (*hana*), they were called Hanafuda, and they become one of the primary gambling devices of twentieth-century Japan. Nintendo was (and still is) the primary manufacturer of Hanafuda.

A Place in the Sun, page 86

"A Place in the Sun" was written by Ron Miller and Bryan Wells for Stevie Wonder. In 1966 it reached number 9 on the U.S. pop charts, and since then it has been covered by everyone from the Supremes to Engelbert Humperdinck. It has also been recorded (in Japanese) by Miki Imai, Keison, and Kiyomi Suzuki for the Japanese market.

The Hanging Bridge Effect, page 112

I can't describe it half as well as Takano Akira did on page 135 of Volume 1. But for those who have joined us late: When one is in a frightening situation, one gets a breathless, heart-drumming feeling, and if a member of the opposite sex is present, one can confuse those feelings for love.

Clean-up Duty, page 146

Although there are janitors in Japanese schools, the primary work of keeping the classroom clean falls to the students who use the room as their homeroom. The jobs are divided equally among the students, but there are always a few students who are willing to work very hard to get out of the relatively easy clean-up duty assigned to them.

Sweet Potatoes, page 152

Yakiimo is a baked sweet potato that is sold by street vendors and is a popular treat in the fall and winter months in Japan.

Kamekichi Kamenne, page 161

Kame is the Japanese word for turtle, and in this one-page manga, the two turtle's names are Kamekichi ("kichi" means happiness and is often the second kanji in men's names) and Kamenne (the "nne" ending is actually the French female name ending, which the Japanese know very well from the legend of Jeanne d'Arc).

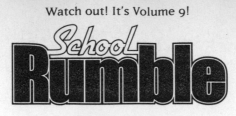

FREE

wallpapers

icons

previews

visit

www.tanoshimi.tv

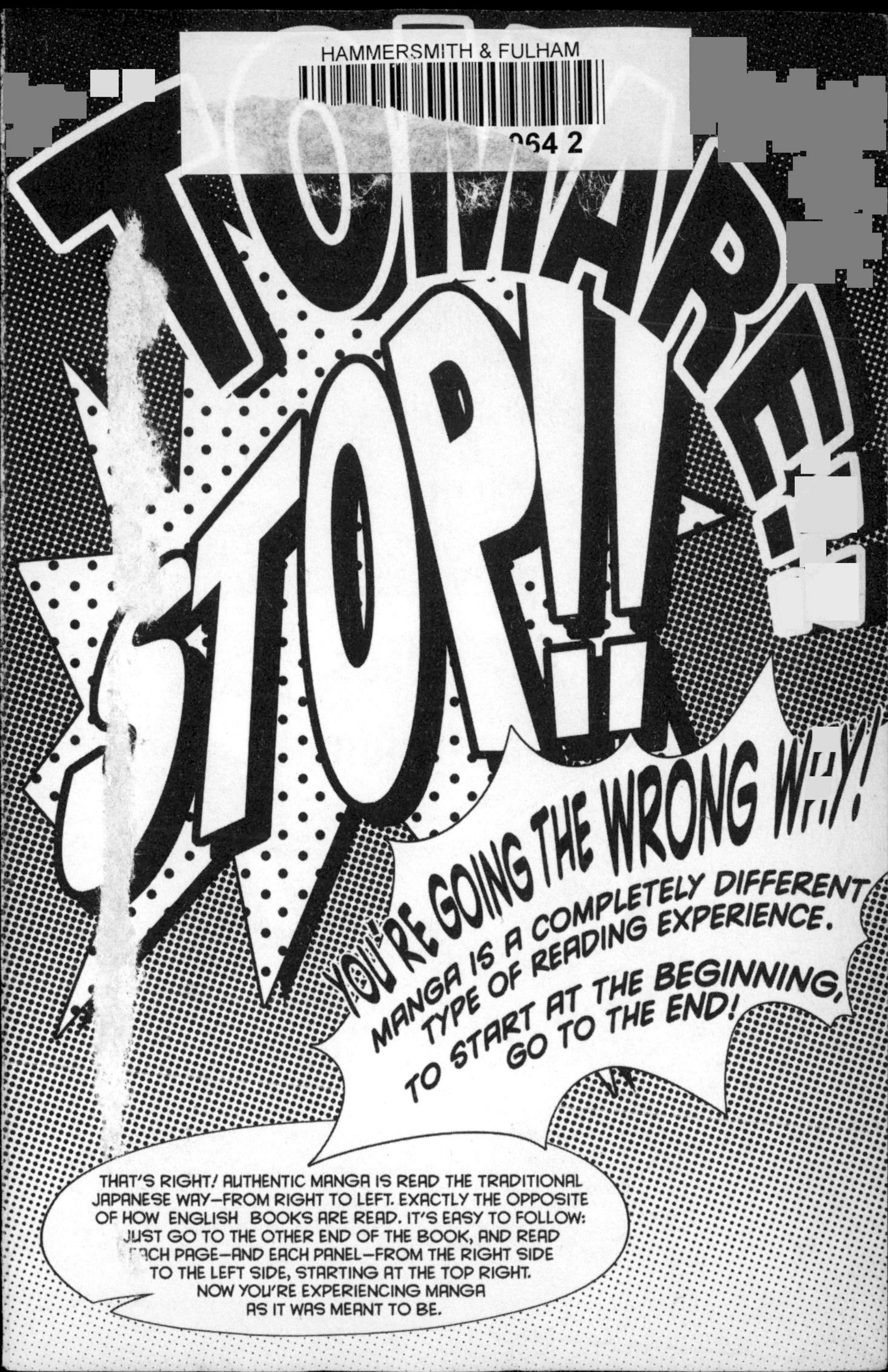
STOP!!
YOU'RE GOING THE WRONG WAY!
MANGA IS A COMPLETELY DIFFERENT TYPE OF READING EXPERIENCE.
TO START AT THE BEGINNING, GO TO THE END!
THAT'S RIGHT! AUTHENTIC MANGA IS READ THE TRADITIONAL JAPANESE WAY—FROM RIGHT TO LEFT. EXACTLY THE OPPOSITE OF HOW ENGLISH BOOKS ARE READ. IT'S EASY TO FOLLOW: JUST GO TO THE OTHER END OF THE BOOK, AND READ EACH PAGE—AND EACH PANEL—FROM THE RIGHT SIDE TO THE LEFT SIDE, STARTING AT THE TOP RIGHT. NOW YOU'RE EXPERIENCING MANGA AS IT WAS MEANT TO BE.